First World War
and Army of Occupation
War Diary
France, Belgium and Germany

46 DIVISION
Headquarters, Branches and Services
Adjutant and Quarter-Master General
23 February 1915 - 3 June 1915

WO95/2666/2

Published by

The Naval & Military Press Ltd

Unit 10 Ridgewood Industrial Park,

Uckfield, East Sussex,

TN22 5QE England

Tel: +44 (0) 1825 749494

www.naval-military-press.com

www.nmarchive.com

This diary has been reprinted in facsimile from the original. Any imperfections are inevitably reproduced and the quality may fall short of modern type and cartographic standards.

© **Crown Copyright**
Images reproduced by permission of The National Archives, London, England, 2015.

Contents

Document type	Place/Title	Date From	Date To
Heading	WO95/2666 46 Div. A & Q Feb'15-July'19		
Heading	46th Division 'A' & 'Q' Branch Feb 1915-Jly 1919		
Heading	War Diary of A and Q Branch Head Quarters North Midland Division from February 23rd 1915 to March 31st 1915 (Volume I)		
War Diary	Boulogne	23/02/1915	24/02/1915
War Diary	Bavinchove	25/02/1915	02/03/1915
War Diary	Oxeleare	03/03/1915	08/03/1915
War Diary	Pradelle	09/03/1915	11/03/1915
War Diary	Sailly-Sur-Le-Lys	11/03/1915	15/03/1915
War Diary	Merris	16/03/1915	31/03/1915
Heading	War Diary Appendices		
Miscellaneous	Indent For Horses. North Midland Division. Appendix II	19/03/1915	19/03/1915
Miscellaneous	North Midland Division Return of Ration Strength Appendix III	20/03/1915	20/03/1915
War Diary	North Midland Division Rations issued March 26th 1915. Appendix IV	26/03/1915	26/03/1915
Heading	War Diary of North Midland Division (Administrative Branch) from April 1st 1915 to April 30th 1915 (Volume II)		
War Diary	Merris	01/04/1915	06/04/1915
War Diary	St Jans Cappel	06/04/1915	30/04/1915
Heading	War Diary of Headquarters 46th (North Midland) Division Administrative Branch. from May 1st 1915 to May 31st 1915 (Volume 3)		
War Diary	St Jans Cappel	01/05/1915	31/05/1915
War Diary	46th Division War Diary of 46th (North Midland) Division (Administrative Branch) from June 1st 1915 to June 30th 1915 (Volume IV)		
War Diary	St Jans Cappel	01/06/1915	03/06/1915

WO95/2666

46 Div. A & Q

Feb '15 – July '19

(2)

46TH DIVISION

'A' & 'Q' BRANCH

FEB 1915-JLY 1919

Confidential

War Diary

of

A and Q Branch
Head Quarters
North Midland Division

From February 23rd 1915 to March 31st 1915

(Volume I)

Army Form C. 2118.

WAR DIARY
or
INTELLIGENCE SUMMARY.
(Erase heading not required.)

Instructions regarding War Diaries and Intelligence Summaries are contained in F.S. Regs., Part II. and the Staff Manual respectively. Title pages will be prepared in manuscript.

Hour, Date, Place	Summary of Events and Information	Remarks and references to Appendices
BOULOGNE February 23rd 1915	Advance Party - Captn DANSEY DAA & QMG and Staff Captain O/Brigade RHA & Motor Cars drivers servants arrived at BOULOGNE at 10 p.m. from FOLKESTONE. Instructions from Base Commandant to proceed to HAZEBROUCK	
February 24th	And report to HQ 2nd Army 2nd Army rptd to 2nd Army Division allotted area near CASSEL. Billeting Area for Division at HAZEBROUCK. Sent advance party to BAVINCHOVE. Proceeded to BAVINCHOVE this morning 2nd	E. Elbert Thomas, invalid and expir
BAVINCHOVE February 25th	Posted as Entraining Officer HAVRE names of Entrainment Entraining Stations. Received from 2nd Army list of Entraining stations — HAZEBROUCK, CASSEL, ARNEKE.	
9 p.m.	Received information that first troop trains arrive in evening	
11.28 p.m.	Detail 1st Batn ELWELL Staff Captain Staff Bn As present As SOMER as Regulating Officer. Supply reached CAESTRE Senior Supply Officer & 3 Bn Supply Officers arrived 2nd	x permit to him as regards deposits in advance
Feb 27th	Reported to 2nd Army for instructions re arrivals 2nd	

WAR DIARY
or
INTELLIGENCE SUMMARY.
(Erase heading not required.)

Army Form C. 2118.

Instructions regarding War Diaries and Intelligence Summaries are contained in F.S. Regs., Part II and the Staff Manual respectively. Title pages will be prepared in manuscript.

Hour, Date, Place	Summary of Events and Information	Remarks and references to Appendices
BAVINCHOVE Feb 28th 3 pm	Following troops arrived :- HAZEBROUCK - 2nd R.F.A. less 2 Btys billeted at MARIE CAPPEL BAVINCHOVE (Ingram) Supply Column " 7th N. Mid'x Derby Regt. less 2 Platoons ... TERDEGHEM " 5th N. Staffs Derby Regt. less 330 O.R. & 6th them " " 6th N. Staffs Derby Regt. less 2 Platoons " " 7th N. Staffs Derby Regt. less 2 Platoons " 8th " " " " " OUDEZEELE G.O.C. and 2 A.D.C's arrived (J.H.D.)	× Complete Strength Officers 27 OR 998 Major General Hon J. Stewart-Worthy Lt. Hon Granby Lt R Stewart Worthy
" March 1st	Following troops arrived 5th Leicester Regt. - Complete Strength Officers 30 OR 990 Yorkshire Hussars One Squadron Strength Officers 6 OR 1143 No 4 Coy Divisional Train Strength Officers 5 OR 80 H.Q. N. Midd'x Derby Brigade & Signal Section " " 5 OR 50 Division attached to 3rd Corps for training. Arranged for 1st R Bde to join 4th Division for training in trenches on March 4th, also for attachment DADAG, GSO 2 Staff & 2nd R & RFA Telephone Communication Established to 2nd Army HQ (JHD)	

Army Form C. 2118.

WAR DIARY
or
INTELLIGENCE SUMMARY.
(Erase heading not required.)

Instructions regarding War Diaries and Intelligence Summaries are contained in F. S. Regs., Part II. and the Staff Manual respectively. Title pages will be prepared in manuscript.

Hour, Date, Place	Summary of Events and Information	Remarks and references to Appendices
BAVINCHOVE March 2nd	Following troops arrived :— Divisional HQ, AQ, RA, HQ, RE, Mobile Veterinary Section. Divisional Cyclist Company Strength Officers 1 O.R. 25 Three Head Quarters in billets in OXELAERE yyd. Strength Officers 8 O.R. 191	HQ arrived at 7pm; no information being sent of their arrival. Some great difficulty. Sleeping boats. One day, in the journey & had to secure houses than was of great assistance.
OXELEARE March 3rd	Following troops arrived :— 1/2nd Field Coy R.E. Strength Officers 6 O.R. 211 1st Field Ambulance Strength Officers 10 O.R. 239 5th Lincoln Regt (2 Platoons) 4th Lincoln Regt (2 Platoons) 4th M.L. Howitzer Brigade returned at STEENWERKE and moves attached to 4th Division Staffs Heavy Battery R.G.A. Strength Officers 5 O.R. 163 yyd.	
" March 4th	Following troops arrived HQ 148 Infantry Brigade (less 1 intelligence) Strength Officers 3 O.R. 109 2nd Field Ambulance Strength Officers 10 O.R. 231 Staffs Heavy B^y (remainder) 4th Leicester Regt (2 Platoons) 6th S. Staff Regt (2 Platoons) 8th 2/D Regt less 2 Platoons Strength Officers 27 O.R. 998 Sanitary Section Strength Officers 1 O.R. 28 4th Lincoln Regt (less 2 Platoons) Strength Officers 29 O.R. 1018	

Army Form C. 2118.

WAR DIARY
or
INTELLIGENCE SUMMARY.
(Erase heading not required.)

Instructions regarding War Diaries and Intelligence Summaries are contained in F.S.Regs., Part II and the Staff Manual respectively. Title pages will be prepared in manuscript.

Hour, Date, Place	Summary of Events and Information	Remarks and references to Appendices
BAYART OKELEARE March 4th	(contd) Ammunition Park (by road) Strength Officer 6 OR 350 R+B Bn – finished by bus & march, made to NIEPPE & to attached to 4th Division also Staff as annexed. JHD	
" March 5th	Yellowing Amps arrived HQ and No1 Lockers Signalling; Strength Officer 2 OR 109 No2 Lockers Signal Company " Officer 1 OR 26 HQ Suri. Field Brigade " Officer 4 OR 24 No2 Coy Divisional Train " Officer 5 OR 59 8th Batts Derby Regt (less 2 Platoons) Strength Officer 30, OR 932 J/Col Elton D.S.O appointed G.S.O1 vice Lt Col. WEBER as Labour Bn JHD	Great inconvenience caused by Signal Company arriving so late – no means of communication being available
" March 6th	Yellowing Amps arrivin HQ Hqrs 1,2,3 Divisional Ammunition Column 5th Lincoln Regt (less 2 Platoons) Strength Officer 29, OR 994 No 4 Labour S.A.C No 5 Battery Regt (330 men) HQ & 2nd Battery 3rd B- R.F.A Complete Strength Officer 29, OR 992 5th S. Stafford Regt Strength Officer 31, OR 990 5th R. Stafford Regt (2 Platoons) JHD	

WAR DIARY
or
INTELLIGENCE SUMMARY.
(Erase heading not required.)

Army Form C. 2118.

Instructions regarding War Diaries and Intelligence Summaries are contained in F.S. Regs., Part II. and the Staff Manual respectively. Title pages will be prepared in manuscript.

Hour, Date, Place	Summary of Events and Information	Remarks and references to Appendices
OXELEARE March 6th	(Cont'd) FLETRE – CAESTRE – METEREN – MERRIS – STRAZEELE – BORRE – from above to complete 9th Div. Received orders from 2nd Army. Attachment of further troops & Staff Officers to Division for training purposes.	
March 7th	Following troops arrived 4th Leicester Regt (remainder) H.Q. ann (H.Q. & 1 Coy) Signal Train 5 & Staff: Rest Mess 2 Platoons 6th S. Staff Regt less 2 Platoons H.Q. Staff: Inf. Brigade & No 3 Section Signal Coy: No 3 Coy: Divisional Train 3rd R.F.A. (remainder) JAP	
March 8th	Following troops arrived 6th R Staff Regt 3rd Field Ambulance 1st R & B & R.F.A., who detrained by arrangement at HAZEBROUCK and proceeded direct to new area. Reform Division has complete except for ATC Amm. Sub. JAP	

(73989) W4141—463. 400,000. 9/14. H.&J.Ltd. Forms/C. 2118/10.

Army Form C. 2118.

WAR DIARY
or
INTELLIGENCE SUMMARY.

(Erase heading not required.)

Instructions regarding War Diaries and Intelligence
Summaries are contained in F.S. Regs., Part II.
and the Staff Manual respectively. Title pages
will be prepared in manuscript.

Hour, Date, Place	Summary of Events and Information	Remarks and references to Appendices
PRADELLE March 9th	Division (also 1"DR/RFA, which Hur) marched to new area. HQ locates at PRADELLE, Infantry along BORRE—MERRIS road, Artillery in north. NCOs & Duty B.M. returned from 4" Division, also Majors ARMITAGE and LEGGE. With Duty B.M. was 5" R.B. Regt and with 5" Leicesters attached Officers following casualties while in the trenches. 5" B.— Leic: Regt Officer killed 1 — Lieut G. AKED O.R killed 1 5" R.B. Regt O.R killed 1, 6" R.B. Regt O.R killed 1 7" R.B. Regt O.R killed 1 (accidentally) GHQ	
" March 10th	Orders to prepare for probable move by motor-bus. Railhead SAIW CHESTRE refilling points in each Brigade Area Ranport in Armitage ammunition remaining in D.A.C.	
PRADELLE March 11th	Orders received 10 a.m to move J Division to SAILLY- sur-la-LYS marched about noon. Have their guns & have surplus Rev behind and any to start rations forward, St Luis histon them centrally. Division marched at noon. Billeting area allotted along ETAIRES — BAC S.T MAUR roads running north Canadian	Only one B" was between there at short Ryhtel & Company men can not Company surplus Rev TC. Divisions not one Tilleuls Frost sufficiency infantry accommodation roomy, Headers and 7" Division being in shelter area
SAILLY-sur-la- LYS	"	

Army Form C. 2118.

WAR DIARY
or
INTELLIGENCE SUMMARY.
(Erase heading not required.)

Instructions regarding War Diaries and Intelligence Summaries are contained in F.S. Regs., Part II and the Staff Manual respectively. Title pages will be prepared in manuscript.

Hour, Date, Place	Summary of Events and Information	Remarks and references to Appendices
SAILLY-Sur-la-LYS March 11"	All transport left in late midnight. Arts feeding to troops satisfactorily. Carried out. Refilling point for next day Le PETIT MORTIER. Divisor moved to be ready to move at one hours notice after 6 a.m. Afterwards changed to 10 a.m. owing to reporting on Lahore arrival.	
" March 12"	Visit by Canadian and 7th Division and managed to fit the Division into our area allotted. Kitts & Derby Brigade ordered to be ready to form 2nd Cavalry Divn. Also 1st Field Ambulance and No 4 Coy. Supply Train — As he	
March 13"	Supplied by this Division — Lawthis CAESTRE (?) 9th RFA joined 2nd Cavalry Division at NEUF BERQUIN. Hrqtrs return from 16.9.10, LD Horses 2966, HD 1088 Appendix I
March 14"	Orders received to move to MERRIS - TROU-BAYARD - LE PETIT MORTIER - BAILLEUL Hutton Area. YMD
" March 15"	Move to MERRIS postponed from 6th Division also from 73rd RFA Heavy Bty ordered to from MERRIS (?)
MERRIS March 16"	Division moved into MERRIS area — H.Qrs at MERRIS Refilling point MERRIS and LE PETIT MORTIER. 3rd Bde RFA and Heavy Battery move cancelled Refilled Coy remained at SAILLY Y.M.D

Army Form C. 2118.

WAR DIARY
or
INTELLIGENCE SUMMARY.
(Erase heading not required.)

Instructions regarding War Diaries and Intelligence Summaries are contained in F.S. Regs., Part II and the Staff Manual respectively. Title pages will be prepared in manuscript.

Hour, Date, Place	Summary of Events and Information	Remarks and references to Appendices
MERRIS March 17th	1/2nd Field Coy reported and billeted at LE VERRIER. Southern portion of billeting area west of 1/16 and Northern area allotted to FLETRE and METEREN.	
March 18th	2nd Br. R.F.A, 2 Br.s Lincs. and 1 Br. and 2 Br.s Staffs Bn. moved into fresh billets being too crowded in area. Salvin Store at CAESTRE for winter clothing being returned. CRE arranged to obtain 3000 sandbags for flooring purposes. Refilling point fixed at School from No 1 NOOTE BOOM for tomorrow.	
March 19th	Commenced returning sheepskins to northern Return of Iron Rations (deficiencies in) sent to 2nd Army. Hours officially return to 2nd Army - 75 hours required. Called for a daily return of strength (casualties of Infantry Units). G.O.C. called in for a report on Major Armitage (late G.S.O.2).	Appendix II
March 20th	Today Strength Return, from 17034, Horses 4046. Staff Infantry Bn. and 3rd Field Ambulance (also motor ambulance) from 1/2 Field by R.E. also D.R.A., A.D.V.S. + G.S.O.3 attached to 6th Division at ARMENTIERES + CROIX DU BAC for instruction.	Appendix III

Army Form C. 2118.

WAR DIARY
or
INTELLIGENCE SUMMARY.
(Erase heading not required.)

Instructions regarding War Diaries and Intelligence Summaries are contained in F.S. Regs., Part II. and the Staff Manual respectively. Title pages will be prepared in manuscript.

Hour, Date, Place	Summary of Events and Information	Remarks and references to Appendices
MERRIS March 21st	ADMS authorized Bry 3rd Corps Ar from a Convalescent Dept at Boulogne. ME DESCATS. YPD	
March 22nd	1 Coy 6/S Staffs sent back from 6th Divn on account of cases of scarlet fever. Were received at Lena Dive Rest Belle to replace Staff Bn in trenches on 25.2.22. G.O.C. authorized ADMS temporary rank of any officer he may select for purpose of examining subject to confirmation when Regular & Territorial Units become mixed or aeroplane Regulation. YPD	2nd Army Lr A/3219
March 23rd	Instructions received for draw "Shorts" for Machine Guns. Casualties 5/S Staffs Wounded OR 2 , 6/S Staffs Regt Wounded OR 1 Sick 5/S Staffs OR 21 YPD	Casualties Wounded 5/S Staffs 2 6/S Staffs 1 Total 3
March 24th	1 man 2/S Bn reported as MANCHESTER Hospital WM sprained arm and broken ankle - (wound to have a man who fell out sick). Telephone to a/cms of 1st per Battalion as to returns to 2nd Army secm has 3 internments per Battalion Casualties 6/S Staffs Killed OR 1 Wounded 2 Sick 6/S Staffs Sick 42 YPD	

Army Form C. 2118.

WAR DIARY
or
INTELLIGENCE SUMMARY.
(Erase heading not required.)

Instructions regarding War Diaries and Intelligence Summaries are contained in F.S. Regs., Part II and the Staff Manual respectively. Title pages will be prepared in manuscript.

Hour, Date, Place	Summary of Events and Information	Remarks and references to Appendices
MERRIS March 25th	Rev. YLEMING (R.C Chaplain) Jones has been sent to LE MONT des CATS hospital.	
" March 26th	Staffordshire Brigade returning from Trenches. As 6th Bure also 1 Battery from each Bde. and Heavy Bty & 60 Yorkshire Hussars & 2 A.A.Cav.Bde. YH AA, QMG attached to 4th Divn also June rehd Bde. (less 5th Lin Regt) and 81 & the Army Res & 170 reservists of Staff. Bde. at present in trenches. Also Bde. Battery from each R.G. RFA and remainder of Yorkshire Hussars. Case of enteric - Spirit - Kerosene at STEENJE - place of burial cases of bromide ypr.	Appendix IV
March 27	Returns drawn for As Army from 16/9/4, Horses LD 2452, HD 1477. Enquiry whom rendered. Completed arrangements for baths for men and washing clothing. Ammunition expended March 21-25: 2nd Line Bde 555, 2nd Staff B4 181 4/Staff B4 160. Total 15 pr. Shrapnel 396; 4.7" Lyddite 74. Casualties. Nil. Ypd	
March 28th	Fighting horses sunned - Yorks. Hussars C2.2, AD 1 R.A SC2.2, B1, LD.2, HD 6 Ammunr. HD 29 New knts C2-9, R1-8, LD.2, HD.2 3	Total horses C2 13 R1 9 LD 4 HD 59 85

WAR DIARY
or
INTELLIGENCE SUMMARY.
(Erase heading not required.)

Army Form C. 2118.

Hour, Date, Place	Summary of Events and Information	Remarks and references to Appendices
MERRIS March 28th	Casualties 5th Lincoln Regt 4 lines wounded OR 1, 5th Lines wounded OR 1. Sick 4 Lines Officer 2, OR 27, 5 Lines OR 36, 8 & RB Regt OR 2.	
March 29th	Capt SOAMES Regimental 5/S.S Coys Regt and Lt GREEN R.A.M.C reported sick - admitted hospital - wounds unknown. Reinforcement reports Lieut ROUEN - 4th R.B. Han: B.C. 2/Lt J.M. SPURRIER and F.M. JOYCE. Casualties 4th Lines wounded OR 1, 5th Lines 4/Leics K. OR 1, wnd OR 2, 8th RB Regt wnd Applies for 28 Travelling Kitchens	Total Casualties D·R K W 4/Lines — 1 4/Leics 1 2 Total 1 — 3
March 30th	Reinforcement Lieut ROUEN Signal Supply Off: OR 11. Sick wastage return for week ending March 27th - A & Q 68 or 4% 5/Lincs Battery Officer 1. L/C PASS reported for duty with Divisional Train. Lt F.P. DAVIS sick. Casualties 4 Lines: wnd OR 2, 5th Lines: K. OR 1, wnd OR 2, 4 Leics: K & O.R 2, 8 R.B / & Battys wnd OR 2 (3) Bathing Arrangements for Staff Divisional Troops.	K. O.R W 4 Lines — 2 5 Lines 1 2 4/Leics — 2 8/R.B.Bn — 2 Total 1 — 8

WAR DIARY
or
INTELLIGENCE SUMMARY.
(Erase heading not required.)

Army Form C. 2118.

Hour, Date, Place	Summary of Events and Information	Remarks and references to Appendices
MERRIS March 31st	Reinforcements Supply train from ROUEN 5/Roths r'Augy Ret Officer 1 Division Divisional Supply Column O.R 12 5/R Staff Regt and S/S Staffs Regt proceeded to BAILLEOL to take over duties of trenches - 2 Officers to go into trenches to night. 3rd Bde R.F.A trained to proceed to LOCRE tomorrow. Divisions incorporated in 2nd Corps from midnight to morrow. Stretcher bearer Bn (Also 5th Leic. Regt) and 8/ Rifle Brigade returned to Division from trenches. yyy	

War Diary
———

APPENDICES

1. Nos: drawing Rations   12.3.15.
2. Demand for horses   19.3.15.
3. Nos: drawing Rations   20.3.15.

War Diary Appendix II

INDENT FOR HORSES.
NORTH MIDLAND DIVISION.

FORMATION.	Chargers		Riding		Draught			Mules L.D.	REMARKS.
	C.1	C.2	R.1	R.2	L.D.	H.D.	PACK		
Divisional Headqrs.	2								To complete Establishment. The present G.S.O. (1) only brought 1 horse.
Divisional Artillery	2 (both 14 stone)		1		7 (a)	6 (b)			To replace horses dead. (a) 2 (b) 3 deficiencies not completed at HAVRE.
Divisional Ammunition Column.						10			8 died or destroyed. 2 for R.E. Explosives Cart.
Divisional Cavalry.			1			1			Died.
Other Units.	1	11	8	2	23				C.1 for Staff Officer. 14 st. 7 lbs. C.2 for Chaplains (2) 6 for Interpreters. 2 up to 14 st. 7 lbs. for Officers entitled to but not yet issued with a horse. 1 to replace casualty. 7 R.2 to Mobile Veterinary Section on increase in Establishment, 1 for R.E. increase in Establishment. 2 L.D. died. 23 H.D. destroyed or died - 12 for A.S.C. Units.
	5	11	2	8	9	40	-	-	

Headquarters,
North Midland Division.

19th March, 1915.

Major-General.
Commanding 1/1st North Midland Divis on T.F.

North Midland Division
Returns of Ration Strength - 20.3.1915.

Appendix III War Diary

NUEF BERQUIN	Men	Horses Light	Horses Heavy	STEENJE	Men	Light	Heavy
N.M.D. Hqrs	69	37	-	Divl Troops II			
5th Notts & D.	1050	45	22	Hqrs Coy a/b	72	10	63
6th " "	1030	54	18	1st R.F.A.	623	439	110
7th " "	1030	49	23 -72	2nd "	634	454	123
8th " "	1033	14	61 -75	Heavy Batty	201	30	110
1st R.a.m.b.	263	14	42	Divl Amm Col	276	39	255
4 Coy a/b	80	10	69	2nd R.E.	216	58	18
Total	4555	223	235	Total	2022	1030	679

MERRIS			
Staff I.B. Hqrs	83	31	4
5th S. Staffs	1032	41	19
6th "	1023	37	21
5th N. "	1027	50	9
6th " "	1016	33	29
3 Coy a/b	93	12	87
3rd R.a.m.b.	276	32	26
Total	4550	236	195

Summary

4555	223	235
4550	236	195
1377	810	170
4530	253	215
2022	1030	679
Total 17034	2552	1494
	1494	
	4046	

Divisional Troops I			
Hqrs n.m.D.	120	54	10
Yorks Hussars	143	159	-
Divl Cyclists	202	-	6
Signal Coy	145	95	-
a/b	31	35	25
Sanitary Sectn	30	-	-
3rd R.F.A.	632	439	110
b R.a.	32	16	4
Hqrs Coy a/b (Baffalo)	42	12	15
Total	1377	810	170

STEENJE			
L+L Hqrs	88	50	-
4th Lincs	1010	47	25
5th "	1020	48	25
4th Leic	1010	47	25
5th "	1020	36	25
2nd R.a.m.b.	288	14	44
2 Coy a/b	94	11	71
Total	4530	253	215

D.J. Wildeblagin

North Midland Division   Appendix IV

Rations issued March 26th 1915.

VIEUX BERQUIN.   ### MERRIS.

	MEN.	L.	H.		MEN.	L.	H.
N+D. Hd Qrs.	71.	28.	9.	Hd Qrs N.M.D.	120.	54.	10.
5th N+D.	1016/998	38.	22.-70	Detention Hosp.	25.	-	-
6th	1026/1030.	54.	18.-21	Signal Co RE.	142.	93.	-
7th	1022/1020.	50.	9.-59	A.V.C.	27.	40.	25.
8th	1011/1031.	13.	48.-61	17th San. Section.	30.	-	-
1st R.A.M.C.	253.	14.	42.	3rd R.F.A.	645.	427.	124.
4 Coy A.S.C.	(95)	12.	63.-6	C.R.A.	33.	17.	4.
	4498.	209.	211.	Hd Qr Co. A.S.C.	55.	12.	15.
				Div. Cyclists.	200.	-	6.

STEENT-JE.

	MEN.	L.	H.	Interpreters.	7	-	-
L+L Hd Qrs.	88.	52.	-	Hd Qrs D.I.B.	73.	31.	4.
4th Lincs. +285.	1000/910	46.	12.-53	5th S. Staffs.	997-1032	41.	19.
5th -do-	1020/990	48.	25.	6th -do-	1013/940.	35.	20.
4th Leicesters.	1020/977	47.	25.	5th N. Staffs.	999/1025.	50.	9.
5th -do-	1020/998	40.	25.-4	6th -do-	1011/1010.	33.	29.
2nd R.A.M.C.	233.	14.	44.	3 Coy A.S.C.	94.	13.	66.
2 Coy. A.S.C.	(90)	11.	72.	3rd R.A.M.C. +53	299.	25.	36.
	4471.	258.	203.	Yorks Hussars.	141.	158.	-
					5898.	1029.	367.

Div. Troops Group II.

1st R.F.A.	575.	362.	157.
2nd -do-	631.+6	456.	121.
Amm. Col.	264.	39.	256.
Heavy Batty	201.	31.	109.
Hd Qr Coy. A.S.C.	40.	10.	33.
	1711.	898.	676.

SUMMARY.

	MEN.	L.	HORSES. H.
	4498.	209.	211.
	4471.	258.	203.
	1711.	898.	676.
	216.	58.	20.
	5898.	1029.	367.
	16794.	2452.	1477.

ARMENTIERES.

2nd N.M. R.E.	216.	58.	20.

27/3/15

121/5/108

Confidential

War Diary
of
North Midland Division
(Administrative Branch)
from April 1st 1915 to April 30th 1915
(Volume II)

WAR DIARY or INTELLIGENCE SUMMARY

Army Form C. 2118.

Hour, Date, Place	Summary of Events and Information	Remarks and references to Appendices
MERRIS April 1st	5/S.Staffs and S/L.Staffs marched from BAILLEUL to NEUVE EGLISE area and took over trenches of 2 Bn & 83rd Bde (5th Div). 6/R.Staffs and 6/S.Staffs and H.Q. Staff Bn. marched to BAILLEUL and billeted there for night. 1st rest and 3rd Bn R.F.A. took over by this division — Refilling Points BAILLEUL and LOCRE. Reinforcements Ammunition Park 14 M.T. Divisional Supply.	
" April 2nd	6/R.Staffs and 6/S.Staffs marched via NEUVE EGLISE to 7/L.D.Regt. and 8/L.D.Regt. marched to LOCRE to take over line from 14th 25th Bde. 5th, 6th L.D.Regt. Artillery between OUTTERSTEENE and BAILLEUL Casualties 5/N.Staffs wounded O.R. 3. Refilling Points Staffs Bde junction of BAILLEUL-ARMENTIERES & NEUVE EGLISE roads. Notts & Derby Bde PLACE PICHON BAILLEUL 3rd Bde R.F.A. Church at LOCRE. Reinforcement left ROUEN at 19.45 — R.F.A. 10 other OR. Enemy report of situation in line — Ch.1:3; Ch.2:9; R.1:12; R.2:1; L.D.23; H.D.2:6; L.D.(Bucks) 3. Casualties at 12 noon: 5/S.Staffs Killed OR 2 wounded OR.2 5/L.Staffs " OR 1 " OR 4	Casualties R. W 5/L.Staffs Regt — 3 Horse Deficiencies Ch.1: 3 Ch.2: 9 R.1: 12 R.2: 1 L.D: 23 H.D: 2/6 Mules: 3 — 77
" April 3rd	5/L, N/D Regts moved to BAILLEUL 4/"S" Leicesters moved to DRANOUTRE to take over trenches from 84 Brigade	Casualties OR K W 5/S.Staffs 2 4 5/L.Staffs 1 4 — 3 6

WAR DIARY or INTELLIGENCE SUMMARY.

(Erase heading not required.)

Army Form C. 2118.

Hour, Date, Place	Summary of Events and Information	Remarks and references to Appendices
MERRIS April 3rd	Rations drawn previous day, Men 17031; Horses - HD 1784, LD 2228. Portion of Divisional Ammunition Column marched to ST JANS CAPPEL. Major T.T. GRESSON took over command of HQ Leicester Regt and Reinforcements left ROUEN - A.S.C. (R.T.) Groups/Coys Ca. 16 O.R.	Appendix I Horses 1, O.R. 30. begins 14
" April 4"	Reinforcements attended 15 pr 1.5" Ammunition expended 15 pr 1.5" heavy Trench Return of Infantry received Casualties 5/s. Staffs knd 2, O.R. 4 wd 1/2 Trench Coy R.E. moved to NEUVE EGLISE. 4th & 5th Leicesters to Kinder (KEMMEL)	Casualties K W 5/s. Staffs – 4
" April 5"	4th and 5th Leicesters moved to BAILLEUL 5th Trench Coy R.E. joined the Division and moved to LOCRE and KEMMEL 1st Field Ambulance moved from VIEUX BERQUIN to LOCRE Casualties 7 M.R. Regt O.R. killed 1, 5 S.R. Regt O.R. wd 1 5/s. Staffs O.R. kd 3, 5/s. Staffs O.R. killed 1 Ammunition expended 15 pr – 16 HD	Casualties K O.R. 7 M.R. Regt 1 – 5th " " – 1 5/s. Staffs – 3 5/s. Staffs 1 – 2 4
April 6"	4th and 5th Leic. Regts moved to DRANOUTRE Divt. HQ, HQ, 8th Divl. Sig. Coy, Divl. Cyc. Coy; HQ 8th Coy Train moved to ST JANS CAPPEL Area - HQ Or Chateau BLANC ST JANS CAPPEL Yorks. Hussars Squadron remained in OUTERSTEENE owing to accommodation required by their being still occupied by 3rd & 5th Divisions	Difficulty in accommodation owing to Inkt of 3rd and 5th Division new occupying, and billets of Division when we have informed that their areas clear

WAR DIARY or INTELLIGENCE SUMMARY

Army Form C. 2118.

Hour, Date, Place	Summary of Events and Information	Remarks and references to Appendices
April 6th ST JANS CAPPEL	Casualties 4th December O.R. wnd 2, 5th Leicesters O.R. wnd 1, 5/S.Staffs offrs wnd 2, 2/Lincoln F.E.GLINGTON, O.R. 1, 7/Notts & Derbys wnd Off 1, 8th R.D. Regt wnd O.R. 3. Ammunition expended 18pdr 1.2 p/gun, 60/pr Shrapnel 4, 15pr R.L.C. 1.3 per gun (16 rounds). Following units now attached to Division:— H/Bty 10th Heavy Bde R.G.A., 115th R.F.A.(4.7") R.G.A., 106th B (60pdr) R.G.A., 1 Section 9.2" Howrs., 57" Coy R.E. T/D. Anti-Aircraft gun detachment. Killed O.R. 1.	Casualties Officers K. W. Officers — Officers K W 4/Leicesters O.R. 2, 5/Leicesters — 1, 5/S.Staff — 1, 7/R D Regt — 1, 8/R D Regt — 3 Total — 1 — 8
ST JANS CAPPEL April 7th	Casualties 8/R D Regt wnd 1-2/Lt J.M.GRAY, O.R. wnd 3, 7/R D Regt killed O.R. 1, 6/R Staff Regt killed O.R. 1, wnd O.R. 1, 4/Leicesters wnd Officers 2 - Lt T. WHITTINGHAM, 2/Lt H.F. PAPPRILL, O.R. 2, 5/Leicesters killed O.R. 1. Ammunition expended 15pr = 50 Shrapnel. T/D Capt. F SOUTHWAITE. A.V.C. appointed temporarily from "Sick"	6/R D Regt — 1 — 3 7/R D Regt — — 1 — 1 6/S Staff — — 2 — 2 4/Leicesters — — 1 — 1 5/Leicesters — — — — — Total 3 — 5 — 6
" April 8th	Casualties 6/R D Regt killed O.R. 1, 7/R D Regt wnd O.R. 4, 6/R D Regt wnd O.R. 1, 6/S.Staffs killed O.R. 1, 6/S Staffs wnd O.R. 1, missing O.R. 1. Ammunition expended. 15pr Shrapnel 4.5 per gun. T/D	K W M 6/R D Regt — 1 — 4 7/R D Regt — — 1 — 8/R D Regt — — 1 — 6/S Scott Ry — — 1 — 6/S Staffs Res — — 1 — 1 Total 2 — 7 — 1

WAR DIARY or INTELLIGENCE SUMMARY

Army Form C. 2118.

Hour, Date, Place	Summary of Events and Information	Remarks and references to Appendices
ST JANS CAPPEL April 9th	Casualties: 4th Leicesters wnd OR 1, 3rd Leics wnd accidentally OR 2. 6/R.B. Regt wnd OR 1, 7th N.S. Regt B.R. K 2, wnd —, 6th N.S. Staffs Killed OR 3 wnd OR 4, 6th N.S. Regt S. Staffs wnd OR 1. Ammunition expended. 15 pdr 1¾/per gun, How 3¼, Anti-aircraft 3. 2 C.A. arrived for Divn HQ. Lectures on Gas Z.B.B.S. 2" B/R.F.A Quaker. Divisional Ammn Col. moved to CROIX de POPERINGHE. 1847 Fuzes shell ammn separate fuzes returned to No. 1 ordnance. C.R.A reports Captain METTRELL returning to Staff B.G. from hospital. Lt SPORRIER joined 4th How: B.G (Reinforcements) Lt. JOYCE joined 4th How: B.G (Reinforcements) 2nd Corps report that 4th Division are facing 2 × 7 Siege B.Gy. JHD	O R K – W 4 Leics → 2 – 3 Leics – – 6/R.B.Regt – – 7 N.S.Regt 2 – 6 S Staffs 3 – 4 6 ℓ Staffs —— 5 – 9 Officers joining Capt Maynard 3rd TB RFA for Sub Lt JOYCE } 4th How: Reinforcements Lt SPORRIER }
April 10th	Casualties 1st Fuca Coy R.E wnd OR 1, 2nd Fuca Coy R.E wnd OR 1. 5th Leics: K.O.R. 2, 6 S. Staffs K.O.R. 1 wnd OR 2, 5 S Staffs wnd OR 3. 6 Hampshire NorfRegt K.O.R 4, wnd OR 3, 7th N.S.Regt wnd OR 1, 8/R.B Regt wnd OR 1. Ammunition expended. 60 pdr gun 1¾, 18 pdr 5½, 4.7 Ship 3½, 15 pdr Q.F. 4. 5" B.L How 2, 13 pr .88. JHD	Casualties O R K – W 1st Fuca Coy 1 – 1 2nd Fuca Coy 1 – 1 5 Leics 2 – 2 6 S Staffs 1 – 3 5 h Staffs 1 – 3 6 h Norf Regt – 4 7 N Regt – 3 8/R.B Regt – 1 ——— 7 – 12

Army Form C. 2118.

WAR DIARY
or
INTELLIGENCE SUMMARY.
(Erase heading not required.)

Hour, Date, Place	Summary of Events and Information	Remarks and references to Appendices

ST JANS CAPEL April 11th	Arrivals Armourial R.A. Ch.3, Ch.2, R.b. LD.21, HD 13
	A.S.C. R,1, HD 5~, R.E. Ch,2, R,1, R1.2
	R.A.H.C. R2.1, HD 5~, Staff B~ Ch,2, Ch,2, LD1.
	Dundee LD 2, HD 3, XB73~ Ch,2 LD 2.
	Chaplain Ch,2, Yorks Arrow R, 3.
	Casualties 4/Linc wnd O.R.1, S/Lincs K.O.R.1 wnd O.R.1
	5/S.Staff K.O.R.2, wnd O.R.1, 6/S.Staff wnd O.R.2, 5/R.D.B&K.R.
	O.R.1, wnd O.R.2, 6/R.9 Regt wnd O.R.2, 8/R.D.Regt K.O.R.1, wnd O.R.1.
	Ammunition Expended 6dpr Shrap.12, 15-pdr .61, 5"BL How: 65"
	Reinforcements L/Cpl BOGEN 2/Lt C.A.SHIELD S/Leutin , 2/Lt HCH CLAY
	6/S.Staff 2/Lieut A.S. HURD
	Captain HEPBURN Maxim Regt temporarily attached 172nd Coy R.E
	brings to home over 55 huts to 5th Division.
	4HD
		Horses
		Ch, 3~ Ch,2, 9, R, 12, R,2,
		LD. 26, HD 26
		Yeom 59.
		
		Casualties O.R.
		                 K. W
		4/Lincs 1
		5/Lincs 1 - 1
		5/S.Staff 2 - 1
		6/S.Staff - 2
		5/R.D Regt 1 - 2
		6/R.D Regt - 1
		8/R.D Regt , -
		          5 - 10

April 12	Ammunition Park moved from ST SYLVESTRE to METEREN- FLETRE 1 mile west of METEREN Second Corps orders division to use the carpenters to assemble huts to S.Bahnhof — difficulties arisen as 2 Corps. Major COKE R.A.M.C Brigadier appointed as commanding 5/A.9 Regt Lt F.G BRUNT 2nd B~ R.F.A returned from sick. Ammunition Expended 6dpr Shrap 4 3/4, 15pdr 7 3/4, 47 August 3. 15pdr 1 1/2, 5"BL How:1/5, 4.x1 howitzer 30	The Corps Front continues as every available Carpenter employed in improving Civic

WAR DIARY
or
INTELLIGENCE SUMMARY

Army Form C. 2118.

Hour, Date, Place	Summary of Events and Information	Remarks and references to Appendices
ST JANS CAPPEL April 12th	Second Corps reports that 2/Lt DICK CLELAND 9th Border Regt joins A 172nd Coy RE. Casualties: 1st/2nd Coy RE wnd O.R 2, 4th Lncs: K.O.R 1, wnd O.R 2, 5th Lncs: K.O.R 1 wnd O.R 2, 5/S.Staffs: K.O.R 1, wnd O.R 1, 5/R.D.R 1: K.O.R 1, wnd O.R 1, 5/R.t.Regt K.O.R 1, wnd O.R 6, 6/R.t.Regt K.O.R 1, wnd O.R 2, YAD	Casualties O R K W 1/7 Coy RE — — 2 4 Lncs — 1 — 2 5/ Lncs — 1 — 2 5/ S.Staffs — 1 — 6 5/ R.Staffs — 1 — 2 6/R.t.Regt — 2 6 — 16
April 13th	2/Lt F.C. MILNER 1/1 Coy Searchlight section rejoins from sick. Capt W.H. McALLISTER HEWLINGS R.A.M.C. to 4th Div. Rest. Lt G.A. BROGDEN R.A & C. joining for duty with 4 mm from 4 Leicesters. Casualties: 4th Lncs: wnd (accidentally) grenade Coy 1; 5th Staffs wnd O.R 1, 6R wnd O.R 1, 5/S.Staffs wnd O.R 2, 5/R Staffs wnd O.R 1, 5/R.t.Regt K.O.R 1, 6/R.t.Regt wnd O.R 3, 6/R.t.Regt K.O.R 1, wnd O.R 3, Shot 4½, Aircraft. Ammunition expended 60 pdr Lyd 2½, 16 pdr 2, 13 pdr 1⅓, 25", 4.7" Shrapnel 4.	4 Lncs — 1 4/ Lncs — 1 5/S.Staffs — — 2 5/R.Staffs — — 1 5/R.t.Regt 1 — 3 6/R.t.Regt 1 — 3 2 — 11

WAR DIARY or INTELLIGENCE SUMMARY

Army Form C. 2118.

(Erase heading not required.)

Instructions regarding War Diaries and Intelligence Summaries are contained in F.S. Regs., Part II. and the Staff Manual respectively. Title pages will be prepared in manuscript.

Hour, Date, Place	Summary of Events and Information	Remarks and references to Appendices
		O.R. O.R.
		K W K W
ST JANS CAPPEL April 14ᵗʰ	Casualties. 1ˢᵗ Fuseliers RE knd 2 OR 1, 4/Lincs K. 2/Lt G. STANILAND OR 1. knd. OR 9. 4/Leics knd Lieut. G.J. HARVEY, OR 1, 5/Leicester knd OR 3, 5/S Staffs knd OR 2, 6/S Staffs knd OR 1, 6/R Regt K OR 1, 8/R/B Regt K. OR 1, knd OR 4. Reinforcements 108ᵗʰ Heavy By OR 2, Divl Ammn Park OR 11 Ammunition expended by fire by day 4.25", 5 lpdr 7.5, 9.2 How 4.7 Shrapt 1.25, 15pdr 2.79, 5" How 1.1, 13pdr.33. JWD	1ˢᵗ Fuseliers 1 - 1 9 4/Lincs - - 1 9 4/Leics 1 - 1 3 5/Leics - - 1 2 5/S Staffs 1 - - 1 6/S Staffs - - 1 - 6/R.R Regt - - 1 4 1 - 3 21
April 15ᵗʰ	Casualties. 1ˢᵗ Field Coy. RE knd OR 6, 172ⁿᵈ Field Coy knd 2 OR 6, 4/Leics: K. OR 1, 5/Leics knd. OR 1 (accidentally) 5/R S Taffs: knd OR 1, 8/R.B Regt knd OR 4. 6/R.B Regt knd on 8.4.15 slightly Lt. T DAVIES. Landing Section of 108ᵗʰ Heavy By to Reinforce by Batt As Bⁿ; Sensing Seʰⁿ of 109ᵗʰ Heavy By An 16ᵗʰ including near Landun An 17ᵗʰ included near Landun. Yorkshire Hussars ordered As home into Rear area Ammunition. An 19 Indian Bde aircraft arrived as BAILLEUL and attacked A. from — Strength Officers 2, OR 4! Daily Ammunition expended 60 pdr by a 1 3/4, Shrapt 5, 13 pdr. 22. 15 pdr . 91. 2ⁿᵈ LS. HWD Junior 1/1ˢᵗ Field Coy RE. JWD	1ˢᵗ Fuseliers - - - 1 172ⁿᵈ Field Coy - - - 6 4/Leics - - - 1 5/Leics - - - 1 5/R.S Taffs - - - 1 8/R.B Regt - - - 4 6/R.B Regt - - - 1 1 - 1 13

WAR DIARY or INTELLIGENCE SUMMARY.
(Erase heading not required.)

Army Form C. 2118.

Hour, Date, Place	Summary of Events and Information	Remarks and references to Appendices
ST JANS CAPPEL April 16th	Squadron Yorkshire Hussars moved to BAILLEUL - ST JANS CAPPEL Road. 4 men of No 19 Section kits except tent & No 10 section 6th Corps in exchange for 4 gone recces from No10 Section. Landing section of 108th Heavy Battery moved to BAILLEUL at night. Ammunition expenses 60pdr Lyd. (Hopkins) 175, Shrapnel 3, 15pdr 2.83, 5" R L Howr 2.37, 13pdr 2.1 Guns in action 60pdr 4, 4.7 4.1, 13pdr 18, Antiaircraft 2, 15pdr 36, 5" How 8, 15" 1 Casualties 1st Field Coy RE kvd O.R 1, 2nd Field Coy kvd O.R 2, 57th Field Coy R.E kvd O.R.1, 172nd Field Coy R.E K:O.R 1, kvd O.R. 8, 4/Leic K.O.R 1, 5/dkLn kvd O.R. 3, 6/2d Staff K.O.R 1, kvd O.R 2, 5/2d Rest kvd O.R 2, 6/2d Rest K.O.R 2, kvd O.R 1, 7/2d kvd O.R 1, 8/2d Rest K.O.R 1 kvd O.R 3, 6/2d Rest (Sydney) kvd O.R 1, gun 6/N.Staff kvd 2/2d R. DAWES Light, Reinforcements: 5/Y.Staff officer 1, O.R. 10 L/Cpl RODEN 16.45 Casualties: R.H.A 9.84 kvd O.R 1, 57 Field Coy kvd O.R. 2, 5/Denies kvd O.R. 2, 4/Leicester K.O.R 1, kvd O.R. 2, 5/Leic kvd O.R. 2, 6/S. Staff kvd O.R 1, 6/2d Staff K.O.R 2, 6/2d Rest kvd O.R 1, 6/2d Rest kvd O.R 8 (slightly at duty) Ammunition expended before dep 25: Shrapnel .5, 4.7 Lyddite 3 Shrapnel 4.5, 15pdr Q.F 3, 5" How 1, 13pdr 3.38. YHD	Casualties D.R K W - - 1st Field Coy 1 - 2nd Field Coy - - 57th " - 1-8 172nd " 1 - 1 4/Leic - - 1 3 5/Leic - - 1 2 6/2 Staff 1 - 2 5/2 R B - - 2 1 6/2 R B - - 2 - 7/2 R B - - - - 8/2 R B - - 1 3 6/2 R B - - - - 1-6-25 Casualties R.H.A - - - 1 57 Field Coy - - - 2 5/Denies - - - 2 4/Leic - - 1 2 5/Leic - - - 2 6/S Staff - - - 1 6/2 Staff - - 2 - 6/2 Res - - 1 9 3 19
April 17th		

WAR DIARY or INTELLIGENCE SUMMARY.

Army Form C. 2118.

Hour, Date, Place	Summary of Events and Information	Remarks and references to Appendices
ST JANS CAPPEL April 18th	Casualties 1st Arty Bg. kna – O.R.1, 5/ Lincs kna – O.R.2 5/ Leics. R.O.R.1 kna – O.R.1, S.S.Staffs kna – O.R.1, 6.S.Staffs kna – O.R.1 6/N.Staffs K.O.R.1, 6/R.Regt K.O.R.4, wnd. O.R.1, 7/R.R.Regt K.O.R.1. Ammunition expended 13 pdr 6, 5" Anti-aircraft 14, 4.7" gun 2.37 Shrapnel 4.25, 15pdr 3.22, 5" How 2. How Bopers left M.17th, How 4.7 joined on 17th Reinforcements arrived 5/N.R. Regt – Officer Capt COLES O.R. 16 from Hospital Reinforcements left HAVRE 1 Guns LH. Shrapnel on 18th – 60 Rds Q, 13 Pdr 18, Anti-aircraft 2 A.T. 6, 15 gun 36, 5" How 8, 1 S/D	Officer K W 1st 4th Leic Bg – 1 5/ Lincs – 2 5/ Leics – 1 S.S. Staffs – 1 6.S. Staffs 1–1 6/N.Staffs 4–1 7/R.R. Regt 1–1 —— 9–7
April 19th	Reinforcements – Left ROUEN M.T. Drivers 40 Casualties 1st Field Coy. R.E. wnd O.R.1, 5/ Lincs O.R.5 5/ Leics. wnd O.R.2, 5/S.Staffs kna O.R.3, 6/S.Staffs kna – O.R.1 5/N.Staff kna – O.R.1, 6/R.Staff kna – O.R.2, 5/Shenwood K.O.R.1, wnd O.R.1 6/ Sherwoods K.O.R.1 kna O.R.2, 8/ Sherwoods kna O.R.1 pw 19 Anti-aircraft train left at night Ammunition expended – Anti-aircraft .5", 4.7" How 3.84, Shrapnel 2.37 15pdr 1.55.	1st 3rd Leic Coy – 1 4/ Lincs – 1 5/ Leics – 1 5/ S.Staffs – 2 6/N.Staff – 3 5/ R.Staff – 1 6/R.Staff – 2 5/ Sherwoods 1–1 6/ Sherwoods 1–2 8/ Sherwoods – 2 —— 2–21

WAR DIARY
or
INTELLIGENCE SUMMARY.
(Erase heading not required.)

Army Form C. 2118.

Instructions regarding War Diaries and Intelligence Summaries are contained in F.S. Regs., Part II and the Staff Manual respectively. Title pages will be prepared in manuscript.

Hour, Date, Place	Summary of Events and Information	Remarks and references to Appendices
St JANS CAPPEL April 20th	Reinforcements. Lt A. ROWEN. L. BEVAN-BROWN. R.A.M.C. for ½ mt Stn. Ammunition expended 13 pdr. 144, 4.7 Lyd. 25, Shrapnel 57, 15 pdr 1.88, 5" How: 1.75. Casualties 1st Field Coy R.E. wnd O.R.1, 4/Lines wnd O.R.1, 5/Lines wnd O.R.5, 5/Shrwds. Sgts & Officers Captain Adjutant N. MOSELEY wnd O.R.2, 6/Staff K.O.R.1, 8/[Regt] K.O.R.5 wnd O.R.1, 5/Shrwds accidentally wounded 2/Lieut T.H.L. STEBBINGS. Six maxim guns arrived for the Division – allotment as follows 5/Lines o 5/Lincs each 1 gun; 4/Lines 1 gun; 5, 6, 7, 8/Sh.d Regt each 1 gun.	Casualties K W OR K W 1st 3 — — — — 1st Field Coy R.E. — — — 1 — 4/Lines — — — — 2 5/Lines — — 1 — 1 5/Shrwds — 1 — — 1 6/Shrwds — — — 5 — 8/Shrwds — — — — — — 1 — 6 – 10
April 21st	Casualties 172nd Field Coy R.E. K.O.R.1, 4/Lines K.O.R.1 wnd O.R.1, 5/Lines wnd Captain T.H. HADFIELD, O.R.1, 5/S. Staff wnd O.R.1, 6/N. Staffs K.O.R.1, 6/Shrwd. Foresters K.O.R.3 wnd O.R.2. Ammunition expended 13 pdr 177, 4.7" Lyd 5.25, Shrapnel 1.62, 15 pdr 5.22, 5" How 2.37. (105 rounds 15 pdr expended on ridge 917 N.E.) Not reported before) 21 O.T.C.P. men to form R.C.H.A., 113 "Heavy Rd" R.G.A arrived & attached. 4. 109"R.P. Later ordered to report H.Q. 5th Corps. POPERINGHE. Lts. A.E. DRYMAN and J. STEVENSON. R.A.P.C. arrived Posted for duty 44th Division. Also Lt F.V. BEVAN-BROWN (R.A.M.C).	172 Coy R.E. — — — 1 — 4/Lines — — — 1 1 5/Lines — 1 — — 1 5/S. Staff — — — 1 — 6/N. Staff — — — 1 — 8/Shrwds — — — 3 2 — 1 — 6 – 5

FVD

(73989) W4141–463. 400,000. 9/14. H.&J.Ltd. Forms/C. 2118/10.

Army Form C. 2118.

WAR DIARY
or
INTELLIGENCE SUMMARY.
(Erase heading not required.)

Instructions regarding War Diaries and Intelligence Summaries are contained in F.S. Regs., Part II. and the Staff Manual respectively. Title pages will be prepared in manuscript.

Hour, Date, Place	Summary of Events and Information	Remarks and references to Appendices

			Officers		O.R.	
			K.	W.	K.	W.

STANS CAPPEL April 22nd

2/Lr G.W. ALLEN 5/Leicesters left BOULOGNE to rejoin from Hospital.
Ammunition expended 13pdr 2, 4.7" 24, 4.62" Shrapnel 25.

15pdr 2.49, 5" How 1.25"

Casualties 4/Lines kmd 2/Lieut W.B. HIRST. 4/Lines K. O.R. 1
kmd O.R. 1, 5/S.Staffs wnd O.R. 1, 5/S.Staffs wnd Major J. LEES
O.R. 2, 5/8 Staffs K.O.R. 1, 5/8.B Regt. K.O.R. 1. wnd O.R. 4
7/B.B Regt wnd O.R. 1, 8/B.B Regt K. 2/Lieut J.R. EDDISON O.R.1 wnd O.R. 8.

		4/Lines	1	—	1	1
		4/Lines	—	—	1	—
		5/S.Staffs	—	—	—	2
		5/8 Staffs	—	—	1	—
		5/B.B Regt	—	—	1	4
		7/B.B Regt	—	—	1	—
		8/B.B Regt	—	—	1	8
			1	2	4	16

8.30pm News received of an attack on French and Canadians north of YPRES
that our from hand retired — Orders given on the information for Transport to be prepared in case of emergency.
Information that German attack was checked the movements from the Germans.
10/5 Lyst R.B. marched to LOCRE and bilieted in the area LOCRE—DRANOUTRE for the night.

April 23rd

Casualties 4/Lines kmd O.R. 1, 4/Leicester K.O.R. 1 wnd O.R. 2
5/Leicester K.O.R. 1 wnd O.R. 1, 5/N.Staffs wnd 2/Lieut A.C.R. DAVIES
5/Sherwoods kmd 4 O.R. 1, 6/Sherwoods wnd O.R. 1, 8/Sherwoods K.O.R. 1
Cpl a Captain R.F.B. HODGKINSON O.R.4.

Ammunition expended 13pdr 44, 4.7" 44, 18pdr 6.62, Shrapnel 1.12
15pdr 2.08, 5" How 3.5"

		4/Lines	—	—	1	—
		4/Leicester	—	—	1	2
		5/Leicester	—	—	1	1
		5/N.Staffs	1	—	—	—
		5/Sherwoods	—	—	—	1
		6/Sherwoods	—	—	1	—
		8/Sherwoods	1	—	1	4
			2	—	3	10

Army Form C. 2118.

WAR DIARY
or
INTELLIGENCE SUMMARY.
(Erase heading not required.)

Instructions regarding War Diaries and Intelligence Summaries are contained in F.S. Regs., Part II. and the Staff Manual respectively. Title pages will be prepared in manuscript.

Hour, Date, Place	Summary of Events and Information	Remarks and references to Appendices
ST JANS CAPPEL April 24th	Lt Col. HARRISON reported as having rejoined 4/ Leicester Regt. Instruction issued re the formation, Major GRESSON having been appointed. Casualties 172nd Coy. kild (Mountain Rest Station) O.R. 1, 4/Leicester kild O.R.1, 5/Leicester kild O.R. 2, 6/S.Staff kild O.R.1, 6/R.Staff kild O.R.1, R. O.R.1, kild O.R.1, 6/Sherwoods kild O.R. 2, 8/Sherwoods wnd O.R. 1. Ammunition expended. 13 pdr 1.72, 4.7" Lyd 4.6" Shrpnl. 88 15 pdr -.91, 5" How 1-. JAMS	P. 3 O.R K.W 172 Coy RE 1 1 4/Leicester 1 2 57 Leicester 2 — 6/S.Staff — 1 6/R.Staff 1 2 6/Sherwoods — 2 8/Sherwoods — 2 7 – 9
April 25th	Reinforcements. Capt. E. LEWIS, 6/S.Staff; Lieut BOULOGNE to rejoin 4th Army Corps annex 1st Br. R.F.A. D.R. 9, 2nd Br. R.F.A 7 3rd Br. R.F.A. 3, 4th Br. R.F.A 1, Grand Amount Cs: 12. Casualties. 4/Leicester wnd. O.R. 2, 5/Leicester wnd O.R.1 6/S.Staff kild – O.R.2/Lieut F.L. STEWARD O.R 2, 8/Sherwoods kild O.R. 14 wnd 2/Lieut R.W. VANN, O.R. 14 Ammunition expended. 13 pdr 3.11, 4.7" lyd 12.87, Shrpnl 7.1 15 pdr 4.25, 5" How 4.75 Reinforcements. 3rd Br. R.F.A Lieut THORNEVILLE Change of Officer Capt COXON Intell Centre transferred to report to 2nd Corps & Lt MALAVLEY this amount to 4th Corps. JAMS	4/Leicester 5/Leicester 6/S.Staff 8/Sherwoods Officers O.R K W 1 14 14 2 – 14 – 19

WAR DIARY or INTELLIGENCE SUMMARY

Army Form C. 2118.

Hour, Date, Place	Summary of Events and Information	Remarks and references to Appendices
ST JANS CAPPEL April 26th	Casualties 1st Field Coy R.E. wnd O.R.2, 5/Leics K.O.R.1, wnd O.R.1, 5/Lincoln wnd O.R.3 (accidentally), 6.S.Staffs wnd O.R.2, 5/R.Staffs wnd O.R.1 (accidentally), 6.R.S.Staffs K.O.R.1, wnd O.R.2, 6/Sherwoods wnd O.R.2, 8/Sherwoods wnd O.R.3 (1 B/slightly on duty), 8/Sherwoods wnd 2/Lieut J.M. GRAY. Ammunition expended. 13 pdr 1:83, 4.7" Lyon S:87, shrapnel 1:62, 15 pdr 0:58, 5" How 2, 2/Army horses arrived. C₂ 13, R₁ 19, R₂ 1, L.D. 13, HD 35, M 12	Casualties Officers O.R K W 1st Field Coy .R.E. — — 5/Leics — 1 2 5/Lincoln — — 3 6/S.Staffs — — 2 5/R.Staffs — — 1 6/R.S.Staffs — — 2 3 6/Sherwoods — — 1 8/Sherwoods — — 1 ————— 1 — 2 — 17
April 27th	Casualties 4/Leics K.O.R.1, 5/Leics wnd O.R.2, 4/Leics wnd O.R.2, 3/Leics wnd O.R.2, 5/S.Staffs wnd O.R.1, 5/R.Staffs wnd O.R.1, 6/R.Staffs K.O.R.1, 6/Sherwoods wnd at dr J. TOLSON. O.R.1, 6/Sherwoods wnd O.R. 29 (killed includes O.R.1 accidentally wnd include O.R. 3 slightly on duty) Reinforcements- Major BARNETT. T.E. 6/S.Staffs. + 2/Lt R.W. DAWES 6/R.Staffs. left Rouen returning from sick. 1 strong trench mortar from D.A.C. Ammunition expended. 13 pdr • 11, 4.7" Lyd 1, shrapnel • 25, 15 pdr 1, 5" How • 12. 2/Lt MARSH and 25 & 60 men and 2 Trench Mortars (1 section) As firm. Ammunition for the try Ammunition YARD	Total horses 97 Casualties Officers O.R K W 4/Leics — 1 2 5/Leics — 1 2 4/Leics — 1 2 5/S.Staffs — — 1 5/R.Staffs — — 1 6/R.Staffs — — 1 5/Sherwoods — 1 1 6/Sherwoods — 1 87 ————— 1 3 17 76

WAR DIARY or INTELLIGENCE SUMMARY

Army Form C. 2118.

Hour, Date, Place	Summary of Events and Information	Remarks and references to Appendices
ST JANS CAPPEL April 26th	Ammunition expended. 13 pdr 1.66, 4.7 Lyd: 7.12, Shrapnel 3.5" 15 pdr 3.11, 6" How 2.37 Reinforcements Lt/ROUEN. 10 Officers, 1 O.R. 4/Lincs Regt, 1 O.R. 7/R.O.B. Regt 6/R. Staffs Regt. Casualties 2nd Field Eng. K.O.R. 1, 172" Coy K.O.R. 2, 1 wnd O.R. 1 4/Lincs wnd O.R. 1, 5/Lincs wnd O.R. 2, 5/S. Staffs wnd O.R. 3, 6/S. Staffs wnd O.R. 1, 5/R. Staffs K.O.R. 1, 5/R. Staffs wnd O.R. 1 (slightly at duty) 6/R.R. Regt wnd O.R. 5, 7/R. Regt wnd O.R. 1 (slightly at duty) 2/BURNLEY Pander 4 Adye Turn YAD	Casualties Officers wnd RAMC w 2nd Field Eng — 1 — 172" — 1 — 4/Lincs — 2 — 5/Lincs — 3 — 5/S. Staffs — 1 — 6/S. Staffs — 5 — 5/R. Staffs — 1 — 6/R.R. — — — 7/R. Regt — — — 4 — 13
April 29th	Capt. J.D. BRACKEN R.G.A (102nd R.M.) appointed G.S.O 3rd Gren 5th Division Capt. D.D. WILSON Casualties Amn. Siphy, at duty on 27th 172 Field Coy wnd O.R. 1, 4/Lincs K.O.R. 1, 4/Lincs wnd O.R. 2 5/S. Staffs wnd O.R. 2, 5/R. Staffs wnd O.R. 1, 6/R. Staffs K.O.R. 1 5/Shenwoodr K.O.R. 1, wnd O.R. 6, 6/Shenwoodr wnd O.R. 3, 5/Shenwoodr wnd O.R. 2 Ammunition expended. 13 pdr .33, 4.7 Lyd: 6.62, Shrapnel 1.75 15 pdr 1.27, 5" How 1 YAD	H.Q. Staff — 1 — 172" Coy R.E — 1 — 4/Lincs — 1 — 2 — 5/Lincs — — — 5/S. Staffs — — — 5/R. Staffs — 1 — 6 6/R. Staffs — — — 3 6/Shenwoodr — — — 2 6/Shenwoodr — — 1 — 3 — 18

WAR DIARY
or
INTELLIGENCE SUMMARY.
(Erase heading not required.)

Army Form C. 2118.

Hour, Date, Place	Summary of Events and Information	Remarks and references to Appendices
ST JANS CAPPEL April 30th	Capt. J.D.D. BRANCKER R.G.A left for 5th Division H.Q Dr. Ammunition refreshed. 13 par. 1.72, 4.7 ryd. 4.39, Shpnel 1.87, 15/14 2.33, 5" How. 2.12 1.G.L began, 1 Telephone began, 6 horses & Harnin. removed for 10th Bde R.G.A 4 Limbers began, 1 Limber Cart, 10 horses, 5 drivers for 192nd Coy R.E Casualties: 1st Field by R.E. wnd O.R. 2, 2nd Fortes Coy wnd Capt B. McGRAITH, 192nd Coy wnd 2, 6/r G.S.M. TAYLOR, O.R.2 4/Limois wnd O.R.1, 4/devon. K.O.R.2, wnd O.R.2, 5-S.Staffs K.OR.1 wnd O.R.1, 5/8 Staffs wnd Lieut. L. CLIVE O.R.1, 5/Sherwoods K.O.R.1 wnd O.R.3 (2 slightly at duty), 8/Sherwoods wnd & sheet F.B. LAWSON, O.R.2. 20th French B.G wnd K.O.R.1, wnd O.R.1 Report on behalf of men on Anny trains of spares skitter when that it tends to hinder the shell extraction in the fighter. Reinforcements to J.A. SHAW O.V.C. promoted from BOULOGNE to join 6 Machine Guns (Nebern) draw retired during march - 4 to 2 BR 4, 2 to Rein. B.n.s	Casualties Officers Men K W K W 1st Fortes Coy - 1 - 2 2nd " " - - - - 192nd " " - 1 - 2 4/Limerick - - - 1 4/devon - - 2·5 5/S.Staffs - - 1 4 5/R.Staffs - - - 1 5/Sherwoods - - 1·3 8/Sherwoods - 1 - 2 French Batt.y - - 1 1 4·5·18

121/5481

Confidential

War Diary

of 46th

Headquarters (North Midland) Division

Administrative Branch.

from May 1st 1915   To May 31st 1915

(Volume 3)

WAR DIARY or INTELLIGENCE SUMMARY

Army Form C. 2118.

Hour, Date, Place	Summary of Events and Information	Remarks and references to Appendices			
			Officers		O. Ranks
			K	W	K	W
ST JANS CAPPEL May 1st	Casualties 4/Linc. K.OR1 wnd OR2, 5/Linc. wnd OR1, 4/Leic: K.OR1 wnd OR3, 5/Leic K.OR1 wnd OR1, 5/S.Staff wnd OR3, 6/S.Staff wnd OR2, 5/R.Staff wnd OR2 (includ 1 Sgt wd. dury) 6/R.Staff wnd OR1 8/Sherwoods wnd OR1, 7/Sherwoods wnd OR1, 8/Sherwoods K. OR2 wnd OR2	Casualties			
		4/Linc			1	2
		5/Linc			–	1
		4/Leic			1	3
		5/Leic			1	1
		5/S.Staff			–	3
		6/S.Staff			–	2
		5/R.Staff			–	2
		6/R.Staff			–	1
		5/Sherwoods			–	1
		7/Sherwoods			–	1
		8/Sherwoods			2	2
					5	19
	Ammunition expended 13 pdr A16, 4.7 Lyd 4.75" Shrapnel 4.12					
	15 pdr 5.52, 6" How 1.87					
	Reinforcements 10th Heavy Bde 4 Drivers arrived 30th April 10 p.m.					
	Fighting Strength Officers 632, OR 17299, Horses 4820.					
May 2nd	Major & Adjutant D.W.L. SPILLER returns to be attached to 5th Divn					
	Artillery on relinquishing appointment					
	Major & Adjutant C.B. GRICE-HUTCHINSON 2nd hh Bde RFA to be attached to	172nd By RFA				
	4th Divisional Artillery					
	Lt C. RUSSELL 27th Divisional Artillery is appointed Adjutant 2nd hh B4th RFA					
	Capt C.H. WALLACE 3rd Divisional Artillery appointed Adjutant 1st hh Bde RFA					
	Casualties 172 Bde By RE wnd OR 3, 4/Leic wnd 2/Lieut K.DALGLIESH					
	O.R.3, 5/Leic wnd Major R.E. MARTIN, OR3, 6/S.Staff K. OR1, wnd OR1	4/Leic			1	1
	6/R.Staff wnd OR2, 7/Sherwoods K.OR1 wnd OR1, 8/Sherwoods K. OR1	5/Leic			–	2
	wnd OR8	6/S.Staff			–	1
	Issues Sniper telescopic rifle. 1 to 4/Linc, 1 to 4/5/R.Staff, 1 to 5/Sherwoods	6/R.Staff			–	1
	Ammunition expended 13 pdr 4.5, 4.7 Lyd 6.5, Shrap 1, 15 pdr 3.72	7/Sherwoods			1	1
		8/Sherwoods			1	8
					2	3	21
5th Hrs 2.12					

WAR DIARY or INTELLIGENCE SUMMARY.

(Erase heading not required.)

Army Form C. 2118.

Hour, Date, Place	Summary of Events and Information	Remarks and references to Appendices
ST JANS CAPPEL May 3rd	Ammunition expended 13 pdr - 27, 4.7 Lydd 4, Shrapl 6.37 15 pdr - 38 Casualties 4/Lines wnd OR 2, 5/Lines wnd OR 7, 4/Leics K.OR 1, wnd 6.R.3, 7/Sherwoods wnd OR 3, 6/S.Staffs K.OR 2, wnd OR 3, 6/S.Staffs K.OR 2, wnd OR 3, 6/ASCStaff K.OR 1, wnd OR 1	Casualties K.OR wnd 4/Lines — 2, 7 5/Lines — , 7 4/Leics 1, 3 7/Sherwoods — , 3 6/S.S.Staffs 2, 3 6/A.SCStaffs — , 1 ——— 4 - 19
" May 4th	Ammunition expended 13 pdr - 88, 4.7 Lyd - 12, Shrapl 2.5 15 pdr 2.5, 5" How 3.75. Casualties 1st Field Coy RE K.OR 1, 5/Lines wnd OR 4, 5/Leic wnd OR No 3, 6/S.Staffs wnd OR 3, 6/N.Staffs wnd OR 1, 6/Sherwoods wnd OR 4, 7/Sherwoods wnd OR 5, 8/Sherwoods wnd OR 1 1.4 pm 200 OR "new men" from different units for service at BAILLEUL in composite Coy; at 2nd Corps H&T. Lt C ASHFORD 6/S.Staff left BOULOGNE to join this unit	1st Fd. Coy 1 5/Lines 4 5/Leic 3 6/S.Staffs 3 6/N.Staffs 4 6/Sherwoods 5 7/Sherwoods — 8/Sherwoods — ——— 1 - 21
" May 5th	Casualties 5/Lines K.OR 1, wnd OR 2, 4/Leics wnd OR 1, S.S.Staffs wnd Capt. W. MILLNER, OR 1, 6.S.S.Staffs K.OR 1, 6/Sherwoods K.OR 1, wnd OR 1, 6/Sherwoods wnd OR 2, 7/Sherwoods wnd 2/Lt A.S.BRIGHT (slightly on duty) Ammunition expended 4.7 Lyd 1, Shrapl 1.37, Shrapl 1.5, 15 pdr - 5 Lieut E.D. ANDERSON 1/N.Staffs appointed Regt. S/N Staffs, and proceed to-day Below rumour Aboukir. Guns stand to cut off Army retreat. 2 Corps Place No 1 Coy Armoured Train Armd Cars from Dyn and Killowe on	5/Lines 4/Leics S.S.Staffs 6/S.S.Staffs 6/Sherwoods 7/Sherwoods 1 - 2 1 - 1 1 - 1 1 - 2 1 - ——— 2 - 2 - 9

WAR DIARY or INTELLIGENCE SUMMARY.

Army Form C. 2118.

Hour, Date, Place	Summary of Events and Information	Remarks and references to Appendices	Officers K. W.	O.R. K. W.
ST JANS CAPPEL May 6th	Casualties 3rd N.M. B. R.F.A. wnd. 2/Lieut C.C. ANSON (slightly at duty) 5/Lincs wnd OR 2, 5/S.Staffs K OR 1, wnd OR 6, 6/S.Staffs accidentally Killed Lieut L.C.B. JOYNSON, accidentally wounded OR 2, 5/N.Staffs wnd 2/Lieut G.H. PAGET, 2/Lieut J.S. DIX K.OR 1 wnd OR 2, 6/2 Staffs accidentally wnd 2/Lt G.H. PAGET OR 1, 5/Shrewsb K OR 2, wnd OR 3, 6/Shrewsb K OR 8 wnd OR 9 Includes 5/slightly at duty. Ammunition expended 13 pdr 28 (8 grns) 4.7" Sgt 41, Shrpnl 18 (8 grm) 15 pdr 95 (36 grm) 5" How 18 (8 grm) Attached over two hour preview a 50 rifle premier to 5th Division during night Sgt.at [?]. 5/L ANNIE 5/Line Regt reserve in open arrest for discharging a rifle 4 wounding Men -Service Corps unconscious. Information that 22 spraying machines and 5 tons of sodium thiosulphate have being dispatched for use against asphyxiating gas	Casualties 37d R.F.A 5/Lines 5/S.Staffs 6/S.Staffs 5/N.Staffs 5/N.Staffs 6/N.Staffs 5/Shrewsb 6/Shrewsb	1 – – 1 – – – – – 1 – 3	– 2 1 6 – 2 1 2 2 2 8 9 12 24
May 7th	Captain A.S. ARCHDALE R.F.A joined 4th How Bn. R.F.A. Major WEBBER joined LAHORE Division Artillery. Casualties 2nd India Cav R.E. wnd OR 1, 4/Lines wnd OR 3, 5/Lines wnd OR 1, 5/S.Staffs wnd 2/Lieut F. WILKINSON. OR 2, 5/N.Staffs K.OR 1, 5/Shrewsb wnd OR 1, 8/Shrewsb wnd Lieut W.C.C. MEETKERK. Use of Copper ware with 4.7 shell sanctioned (Copper hr 26 SWG) Sided Bagmet persecpts All be 48 for R.A. Ammunition expended 13 pdn 30 (18 grm) 4.7" Sgnc 39. Shrpnl 47 (8 grm) 15 pdr 72 (36 grm) 5" How 19 (8 grm).	1st Indian Cav. 4/Lines 5/Lines 4/Lines 5/S.Staffs 5/N.Staffs 5/Shrewsb 8/Shrewsb	– 1 – 1 – 2 2	1 3 1 1 2 1 – 2 2 9

WAR DIARY
or
INTELLIGENCE SUMMARY.
(Erase heading not required.)

Army Form C. 2118.

Hour, Date, Place	Summary of Events and Information	Remarks and references to Appendices

ST JANS CAPPEL May 8th	Reinforcements 5/Shwoods 2/Lieut G.B. ROBOTHAM
	4/Linc Lt W.A. FOX, Lieut W. HALL, 5/Linc 2/Lt D.F. UNDERWOOD
	4/Linc 2/Lt R.S. GREEN, 2/Lt C.B. PEAKE, 5/Linc 2/Lieut L.H. PEARSON.
	5/Linc Major R.E. MARTIN returned from sick
	4/Linc 2/Lt C.B.R. PENNELL returned from wounded
	5/Shwoods Lt F.W.D. JONES (on 2ndtary) G/S. Staff 2/Lt C. ASHFORD from sick
	6/N. Staff 2/Lt M.T. NEWTON (on 2ndtary) Capt. J. JENKINSON from Hospital
	Capt. A.W. STACK (from hospital). Lt J.I. DOBSON, 9/Shwoods on 9th inst.
	6/S. Staff Rgt. 2/Lt DARRY, 2/Lt H.A. JOWETT
	Returning Reinforce to ENGLAND – An 2nd Corps H.Q. O/2.
	to Rev. Army.
	2/Lt C.H. PEARSON with composite Coy.
		Casualties O.R
		              K W
		4/Linc 1 - 3
		4/Linc 4
		5/Shwoods 3
		8/Shwoods 2 - 1
		5/N. Staff 3
		               6 - 11

	Casualties 4/Linc K. OR 1 Wnd OR 3, 4/Linc Wnd OR 4, 5/Shwoods Wnd OR 3, 8/Shwoods K. OR 2 Wnd OR 1, 5/N. Staff Wnd OR 3 (1 accidental) Ammunition expended 13 pdr 43 (18 pdr) 4.7 Lyca 11 Shpnl 36 (8 gun) 15 pdr 159 (36 gun) 5" How 18 (8 gun) .	Officers O.R K W K W 1st Field Coy 1 - 2 17th 2 - 3 4/Linc 1 - - 5/Linc - 2 6/N. Staff 5/Shwoods 8/Shwoods 1 — 12
May 9th	Two short rifles fitted with telescope received & allotted 1 to 5/Linc 1 to 8/Shwoods. Divisional Cyclist Company proceed to billets in LOCRE–KEMMEL road Heller M19 d 4.4 as Mobile Reserve. Ammunition expended 13 pdr SI (8 gun 18) 4.7 Lyd 79 (gun 8) 15 pdr 113 (8 gun 36) 5" How 2 (gun 8)	

WAR DIARY or INTELLIGENCE SUMMARY

Army Form C. 2118.

(Erase heading not required.)

Instructions regarding War Diaries and Intelligence Summaries are contained in F.S. Regs., Part II. and the Staff Manual respectively. Title pages will be prepared in manuscript.

Hour, Date, Place	Summary of Events and Information	Remarks and references to Appendices
ST JANS CAPPEL May 9th	Casualties: 1st Field Coy R.E. knd. OR 1, 172nd Field Coy knd. OR 2 4/ Lincs. wnd. OR 1, 4/ Leicesters wnd. OR 3, 5/ Leics. wnd. OR 1, 6/ R. Staffs wnd. OR 1, 5/ Sherwoods wnd. OR 1, 8/ Sherwoods wnd. 2/Lt J.V. EDGE OR 2. Trench Strength for May 8th 9 Offrs RCO's Men 1750.5" Horses 480.8 Horses received today 9. 6th May. Ch.1, Ch.2 7, L.D. 38, H.D. 22, Mule L.D. 6 (71.74) from 12th May (Capt NEWTON No B3" GOR for work in information area) at Ecle des Arts. Six Officers and 7 men are to attend the 17th Field Ambulance ARMENTIÈRES	Appendix I
May 10th	Reinforcements: Information that Capt. B. McGRATH has been invalided to England. Capt A.L. ASHWELL & 2/Lt W.H. HOLLINS 8/Sherwood Foresters Reinforcements from BOULOGNE do rejoin tn. day from hospital. 4800 Marks for apprehending spies received treasures as Hosp. each Sept 13th 1440, R.E Coy 120 Casualties: 172nd Field Coy. (attached from RFA) knd 2/Lt F.J. MULQUEEN 4/ Leics K. 2/Lt A.C. CLARKE, OR 1, wnd OR 13. 5/ Leics knd. OR 6. 6. S.S. Gffs wnd OR 16, 6/ Sherwoods wnd. OR 3, 8/ Sherwoods wnd. 2 OR 6, 6. S.S. Gffs wnd OR 1, G.N. Staffs K. OR 1 Ammunition Expended. 13 pdr 67 (18 gun) 4.7 Lyd 21 Shrapnel 5" (8 gun) 15 pdr 67 (36 gun) 5" How 11 (8 gun) Sent in return of ACPWen recommended for Russian decoration	Casualties Officers OR K W K W 172nd Coy RE 1 — 1 - 13 4/ Leics 1 — - 6 5/ Leics — — - 16 5/ Sherwoods — — - 3 6/ Sherwoods — — - 6 8/ Sherwoods — — 1 - 6/ S Staffs — — 1 - 6/ N Staffs — — - - _____ 1 - 1 - 46 Horses rec Ch 1 Ch 2 7 L.D 38 H.D. 22 Mule 6 Total 74

WAR DIARY
or
INTELLIGENCE SUMMARY.
(Erase heading not required.)

Army Form C. 2118.

Hour, Date, Place	Summary of Events and Information	Remarks and references to Appendices			
			Officers	OR	
			K	W	K	W
St JANS CAPPEL Aug 11th	Ammunition expended 13pdr 16 (4 guns 18), 4.7" Lyon 29 Shrapnel 9 (4 guns 8)	Casualties				
	15 pdr 224 (36 guns) 5" How 32 (4 guns 8)	172nd Coy			1	
	33 Red Very lights received (116 coast R.L.)	4/Lincs		1	3	6
	Casualties 172nd Tunn Coy R.E. knd OR 1, 5/Lincs knd OR 1, 5/Lincs	5/Lincs				10
	knd OR1, 4/Lincs K Capt H.MAYLOCK OR 3, knd 2/Lt G.E.F. RUSSELL OR10 5/Shenwoods K	4/Lincs				2
	5/Lincs K OR1 knd OR 2, 5/Shenwoods K OR 2 and OR 1. 6/Shenwoods K	5/Lincs				2
	2/Lt H.F.SEVERNE knd OR2, 7/Shenwoods K OR1 knd OR 3 (1 slightly at duty)	6/Shenwoods	1		1	3
	8/Shenwoods knd OR1, 6/S.Staffs K OR1, 6/R.Staffs knd OR 2.	7/Shenwoods			1	
	5/Shenwoods in Dumont at N20 b 5.5, + 15" into farms near	6/S.Staffs				2
	Midland Division designated 46" (North Midland) Division	6/R.Staffs				
	Staffs B" - 137" Brigade, Linc + Leic B" - 138" B", R.M.P. Beds B" - 139" B",		2	1	7	25
	also 46th Annual Route, Signal Coy, Supply Col., Army Coy. Sanitary section					
	No change in designation of RA + Engineer Medical Units					
St JANS CAPPEL Aug 12	Reinforcement 2nd Lieut J.P. DAVIES. A.S.C. continue to embark	2/Field Coy				1
	for France Ao report this event. Capt G.H. SOAMES Bays 5/S. Staff left BOULOGNE	4/Lincs				6
	Casualties 2/Field Coy knd OR 1, 4/Lincs K OR 1 knd OR 1,	5/Lincs			1	3
	5/Lincs knd OR 6, 5/Lincs K OR 1 knd OR 3 (1 slightly at duty)	5/S.Staff				2
	6/S.Staffs K OR 1 knd OR 2, 6/R Staffs K OR 1 knd OR 2, 5/Shenwoods	6/R.Staff			3	2
	knd OR 2, 6/Shenwoods K OR 1 knd OR 13 (2 slightly at duty)	5/Shenwoods				2
	7/Shenwoods K OR 1, knd OR 3 (1 slightly at duty)	6/Shenwoods			1	13
	Ammunition expended 13 pdr 25 (18 guns) 4.7 Lyon 7 Shrapnel 55	7/Shenwoods			1	3
	(8 guns) 15 pdr 152 (36 guns) 5" How B (8 guns)				8	33

Army Form C. 2118.

WAR DIARY
or
INTELLIGENCE SUMMARY.
(Erase heading not required.)

Instructions regarding War Diaries and Intelligence Summaries are contained in F.S. Regs., Part II. and the Staff Manual respectively. Title pages will be prepared in manuscript.

Hour, Date, Place	Summary of Events and Information	Remarks and references to Appendices
ST JANS CAPPEL May 13	Ammunition expended 13 pdr 15 (18 pdr) 4.7" Lyon 39 Shrapnel 64 (Smm 8) 15 pdr 42 (5mm 36) 5" How. 4 (4mm 8). Casualties 1st Field Coy RE k. nil OR 1, 4/ Lincs k. nil OR 2 5/ Lincs k. nil 2/Lt H SHEEL, OR 2, 5/S.Staffs K OR 1 - k. nil OR 1, 6/ Sherwoods k. nil OR 6, 7/ Sherwoods k. nil OR 2, 5/S.Staffs K OR 1, 5/N.Staffs k. nil OR 4 (incidentally) 6/N Staffs k. nil 2/Lt H.W. BECK OR 2. Lieutenant C.C. RUSSEL 27th Bgd Artillery reported as Adjutant 2/N.M.B. of R.F.A. vice Major C.B. GRICE- HUTCHINSON to 4th Division to take effect from this day's date. 25 mm 13 pdr incendiary shells were an experienced trpmt.	Casualties Officers O.R. K. W. K - W 1st Lincs Coy — — 1 — 4/ Lincs — — — 2 5/ Lincs — — 1 — 2 6/ Sherwoods — — — 6 7/ Sherwoods — — 2 — 1 5/ S.Staffs — — 1 — 1 5/N Staff — — — 4 6/N Staff — — — — 1 - — 2 2 - 1-20
May 14"	Casualties Yorks Hussars k. nil OR 1, 4/ Lincs K OR 1, k. nil OR 1 ⊕ 5/ Lincs K OR 2 k. nil OR 1, 4/ Lincs missing OR 1, 5/Sherwoods N OR 2 6/ Sherwoods k. nil OR 1, 7/ Sherwoods k. nil OR 2, 5/S Staffs K OR 1, k. nil OR 2 5/N Staffs K OR 2 (1 accidentally) Cypher used supplied for 4.7" shell Ammunition expended 13 pdr 123 (5mm 18) 4.7" Lyon 34 Shrapnel 31 (5mm 8) 15 pdr 102 (5mm 36) 5" How. 17 (8mm 8). Some 3 own A. A. men in trenches sanctioned owing to inclement weather	Yorks Hussars — — — 1 4/ Lincs — — 1 - 10 5/ Lincs — — 2 - 1 4/ Lincs — — — 1 5/ Sherwoods — — 2 - 1 6/ Sherwoods — — — 1 7/ Sherwoods — — — 2 - 5/ S Staffs — — 1 - 2 - 5/N Staff — — — 2 8 - 14 - 8 - 14 - 1

WAR DIARY
or
INTELLIGENCE SUMMARY.
(Erase heading not required.)

Army Form C. 2118.

Instructions regarding War Diaries and Intelligence Summaries are contained in F.S. Regs., Part II. and the Staff Manual respectively. Title pages will be prepared in manuscript.

Hour, Date, Place	Summary of Events and Information	Remarks and references to Appendices			
			Officers	O.R.	
			K. W.	K. W.	
ST JANS CAPPEL May 15th	Casualties 2n Cyclist Coy and 2/Lt A.P.F. HAMILTON (8/Sherwoods)	8/Sherwood (8/Sherwood)	Cyclists	- 1	- -
	8/Sherwoods 172nd Coy R.E. and O.R.1 4/Leics K. and O.R.1 5/Leics wnd O.R.1	172 Coy	-	1	-
	4/Leics K. OR 1 wnd OR 1 5/Leics wnd OR 3, 5/S.Staffs K. Lt H.W.M. PARR	4/Leics	-	-	1 -
	wnd OR 1, 5/N.Staffs wnd 2/Lt K.W.G. MEAKIN OR 2, 5/Sherwoods K. OR 1	5/Leics	-	-	1 - 3
	wnd OR 10, 7/Sherwoods wnd OR 3, 2/Trick Amb. K. OR 1	4/Leics	-	-	1 - 1
	Ammunition expended 13 pdr 2s — (Serm 18), 4.7 Lyed. 12 Shupnel 4 b (Serm 8)	5/Leics	-	-	- 3
	15 pdr 79 (Serm 36) 5" How 24 (Serm 8).	5/S.Staff	-	-	- 2
	18/Brew 5/Sherwoods arrived. Lt & P. DAVIES A.S.C. left HAVRE	5/N.Staff	-	1	3 - 70
	Lt SMITHSON and 19 hour (Bastern Trench Mortar Bty) reported and attached to	5/Sherwoods.	-	-	- 3
	Notts Div. Brigade.	7/Sherwoods	-	-	- 1
		2 Field Amb	-	-	1 -
			1 - 2 - 6 - 23		
May 16th	Casualties. 5/N.Staffs wnd OR 2, 4/Leics K. Capt A.C. COOPER OR 1,	5/N.Staffs	-	-	- - 2
	5/Sherwoods wnd Capt H.J. COLES, 7/Sherwoods K. OR 1, wnd OR 6,	4/Leics	-	1	1 - -
	8/Sherwoods wnd Capt A.C. ASHWELL (Slightly at duty).	5/Sherwoods	-	-	- - 1
	Incendiary Shells thrown over An R.H.A. Ammn Cn (3rd Cav Bde).	7/Sherwoods	-	-	1 - 6
	Ammunition expended - 13 pdr 5 (Serm 18), 4.7" Lyed 5"-3, Shupnel 79	8/Sherwoods	1	-	- -
	(Serm 8) 15 p dr 90 (Serm 36), 5" How 10 (Serm 8).				
	Reinforcements 3) 2/Lt N.L. HINDLEY & 2/Lt G.G. ELLIOTT 8/Sherwood Forest		1 - 2 - 2 - 8		
	2/Lt J.R. LEESON 4/Leicester Regt.				

WAR DIARY
or
INTELLIGENCE SUMMARY.
(Erase heading not required.)

Army Form C. 2118.

Instructions regarding War Diaries and Intelligence Summaries are contained in F.S. Regs., Part II and the Staff Manual respectively. Title pages will be prepared in manuscript.

Hour, Date, Place	Summary of Events and Information	Remarks and references to Appendices
ST JANS CAPPEL May 17th	Reinforcements 2/Lt R.C.S. BENNETT 5/Sherwood Foresters reported for duty pending training. Casualties Cyclists had - OR 1, 3rd Bde R.F.A. had - OR 2, 5/S.Staff and 2/dt S.P. SMITH OR 1, 5/N. Staff had - OR 1, 4/ Leics had - OR 1, 5/ Leics H. OR 1 had Capt J. CHAPMAN, 2/Lt C.W. SELWYN, OR 2, 5/Sherwoods had OR 3, 8/Sherwoods had Lt F. H. KIRBY, OR 1, Ammunition expended 13 pdr 45 (16 June), 4.7" Lyd: 29 Shrpnl 19 (8 June) 15 pdr 45 (36 June) 5" How 23 (3 June)	Casualties K. W. K. W. M Cyclists - - - - 1 3rd Bde R.F.A - - - - 2 5/S. Staff - - - 1 - 5/N. Staff - - - 1 - 4/ Leics - - - 2 2 5/ Leics - 2 - - 3 5/ Sherwoods - - - 1 - 8/ Sherwoods - - - 1 - 4 12
May 18th	Major A.E.R. IND appointed 2nd in command 6/N. Staff. — Capt G.H. SOAMES late Adj: 5/S. Staffs: As 2nd in 1/W. Yorks Regt. Casualties 4/ Leics missing OR 1, 6/Sherwoods had OR 1, 8/Sherwoods had OR 1. Second Corps amma Park in further raise of 03 pdr, 15 pdr, + 4.7" Lyddite will be made from Parks at Raisheim. Ammunition expended 13 pdr 2nd 4.7" Lyddite 1, Shrpnl 2 (Guns 8), 15 pdr 19 (Guns 36), 4.5" How 10 (Guns 8) Reinforcements Left RODEN 5/ Lancers 2 Officers, Field Ambulance 2 OR Yorks Hussars 1 OR. Rev. Stanley Bishop - Wesleyan Chaplain granted 8 days leave May 24th — 31st.	Casualties 4/ Leics - - - 1 - 4/ Leics - - - 1 - 6/ Sherwoods - - - 1 - 8/ Sherwoods - - - 1 - 3 - 1

WAR DIARY
or
INTELLIGENCE SUMMARY.
(Erase heading not required.)

Army Form C. 2118.

Hour, Date, Place	Summary of Events and Information	Remarks and references to Appendices

St JAN'S. CAPPEL May 19th	Orders received to select officers & command 4 Howitzer Regts and 6/N Staff Bde – no Regular officers being available.
	Casualties 5/Leic R. OR 1, 5/S Staff R. OR 1, 6 S Staff wnd. OR 7
	6/N Staff K. OR 1, wnd. OR 4 (2 acc. incl dy) 8/Sherwoods wnd.
	2/Lt G.W. FOSBERRY, OR 3.
	Ammunition expended 15pdr - 26 (fuses 36).
	Reinforcements left BOULOGNE 5/Leic Rs 2 officers
	Scale of ammunition allowed. 2.75" as required, 13pdr 2, Anti-aircraft no restn,
	15pdr 3, 15pdr QF. As reqd., 4.5" How 3 of which 1 may be HE.
	4.7" 8 of which 5 may be HE, 60pdr 4 & gas. Shrapnel as reqd.
	5" How 2, 6" How 3 of which 1 may be HE, 9.2" How & 15" only under Army permission.
		Amm. Officers
		         K.W
		5/Leics 1 – 1
		5/S Staff 1 – 1
		6/S Staff wnd – 7
		6/N Staff wnd 1–4
		8/Sherwoods – 3
		         1 ── ──
		         1 – 3 –14

" May 20	Approval given for Capt SOMMES. Adjutant 6/S.Staff to command temporarily 6/N Staff: Rest Brit Capt Anderson in hospital. Casualties 5/Leics K. OR 1 und. OR 1, 4/Leic. K. OR 1 wnd OR 1, 6/Sherwoods K. OR 1 und. OR 5 Ammunition expended 13pdr 17 (16 fuses) 4.7" Lyd 1, Shrap 1 (8 fuses). 15pdr 23 (36 fuses) 5" How 14 (fuses 8). Reinforcements RE 1 OR, Ammn 22 OR A.S.C., RE 7 OR Ammn left ROUEN for the Division. Ammn 62 Ammn left ABBEVILLE	

WAR DIARY
or
INTELLIGENCE SUMMARY.

Army Form C. 2118.

Place	Date	Hour	Summary of Events and Information	Remarks and references to Appendices
ST JANS CAPPEL	May 25		Morning trench arrived. Ch, 3, Ch, 2, 5, R, 6, LD 48, German mine exploded in one of our trenches, burying about 30 men. Casualties not yet reported.	Ch, 3, Ch, 5, R, 6, LD 48, 6 2
"	26		1st Div. Cav. R.E. moved with others at ST JANS CAPPEL for 10 days rest. Reinforcements left HAVRE 6/N Staff. Lt Col. A.C.B. IND. Sentence on 8327 9º BIRD 5/S Staff. Rest for "Sleeping on Post" commuted to 2 Yr IHL. Casualties 3rd B R.F.A wnd OR 1, 1st Fris. Cav. K Lt D.E. GOSLING, wnd OR 1, 5/ Lincs K OR 2 wnd C. Capt H I ROBINSON, Lieut E DYSON (slightly ad duty) OR 23, missing OR 2, 6/ Shrewoods wnd C. OR 1, 7/ Shrewoods wnd OR 1, 5/S Staff K OR 1, wnd OR 3, 6/S Staffs K OR 1, S/N Staff wnd OR 2, K OR 1 wnd OR 1 - A certain Casualties during week - 5/ Shrewoods 6 14, 2 OR wnd 2 1, M 16th OR wnd 2, M 18th OR wnd #1, M 17th OR wnd 1. Major E S.COKE 5/ Shrewoods ordered to proceed to take over command of 2nd R.S. K.O.S.B. Lt Col A.C.B. IND 6/N Staffs arrived. Ammunition expended 13 part 33 (16 pdr), 4.7 Hyds 1 (6mm B) 15 pdr 251 (6mm 36) 5" How 24 (6mm B) — Major COKE left at 11:30 for 2/K.O. R.S.	knar K w. K w m 3rd RFA, 1 Frisley 1 - 1 - 5/Line 2.8.43- 6/Shrwds 1 - 7/" 1 - 5/S Staff 11-3- 6/S Staff 1 - - 5/N Staff 1-1- 5/Shrwds -5- 1-2- 11:36
"	26		Orders received that all drafts to be returned to 30th May. Report sent about 2nd 25%. have been returned. Ammunition expended 15 part 4 (36mm) 5" How 1 (6mm). Amount of ammunition allowed are now 6" gun Hyds 3, Shrapl: 3 per Casualties 2nd Fusiliers K OR 1, 4/ Lincs K OR 2, wnd OR 1, 5/ Lincs wnd OR 3, 6/ Shrewoods K OR 2, wnd OR 1, 5/S Staff wnd OR 2, S/N Staff wnd OR 6, 6/N Staff OR 1 (accidentally)	

WAR DIARY or INTELLIGENCE SUMMARY

Army Form C. 2118.

Place	Date	Hour	Summary of Events and Information	Remarks and references to Appendices
ST JAMES CHAPEL	May 23		Casualties 5/S.Staffs wnd OR 1, 6/S.Staffs K. OR 1, wnd 2, Lt G.H. SMITH, OR 1, 5/N.Staffs wnd 2, 2/Lt C.E.H. LOXTON OR 2, 4/Lincs wnd OR 2, 4/Leics wnd OR 2, 5/Sherwoods wnd OR 2, 4/Sherwoods wnd OR 2 (1 dying of wounds). Ammunition expended. 13 pdr 49 (16 gun), 4.7" shrap 38 Lyd 38 (8 gun), 15 pdr 110 (36 gun), 5" How 53 (Reform)	
"	24th		Casualties 4/(How) R.M. RFA wnd OR 1, 5/S.Staffs wnd OR 1, 6/S.Staffs wnd OR 1, 5/N.Staffs wnd OR 1, 4/Leics wnd OR 2, 2/Lt G.H.MARRIS OR 1, 4/Leics wnd OR 2, 5/Sherwoods wnd OR 5, 8/Sherwoods K OR 2, wnd OR 2. Ammunition expended 13 pdr 3 (8mm 16), 4.7" Lyd 9, shrap 23 (8gun), 15 pdr 63 (8mm 36), 5" How 10 (8mm 8). German gas attacks at 4 am much the respirators issued to provide protection for every firearm being 4 feet narrow 6 in (2 to 5" sides) + 800s diminished. Had in 5th Army letters to the effect that these respirators have to be on haversack day & night & they must be practised in being them on. Reinforcement 7 OR Gunners BAILLEUL at 14.30 Ammunition.	
	25		Casualties 6.S.Staffs wnd OR 3, 5/N.Staffs wnd OR 1, 4/Lincs wnd OR 2, 4/Leics wnd OR 1, 5/Sherwoods wnd OR 4, 8/Sherwoods wnd OR 2. Appointment of Major G. A LEWIS to command command of 5/Sherwoods from 22nd inst (inclusive). Ammunition expended. 13 pdr 20 (8mm 16), 4.7" Lyd 67 shrap 8 (8mm 36), 15 pdr 202 (8mm 36), 5" How 11 (8). Decision from AA arthur 25% blankets ineffective but blanket wagons to be returned by Inns. Reinforcement 2/4 Leics Coy 5 OR, 1/Trench bay 2 OR, 1/Queens Rwe 1 OR.	

WAR DIARY or INTELLIGENCE SUMMARY

Army Form C. 2118.

Place	Date	Hour	Summary of Events and Information	Remarks and references to Appendices
ST JANS CAPPEL	Aug 26		Casualties: 6/S.Staffs wnd OR 1, 6/N.Staffs wnd OR 1, 4/Lincs K OR 1, 4/Lincs K OR 1. 6/Sherwoods wnd OR 1, 8/Sherwoods K OR 1, wnd Capt. J.K. LANE, OR 1. Ammunition expended 13 pdr 6, 4.7" Lyd: 6, Shrapnel 9, 15 pdr 24, 13 pdr 15. Congregational Chaplain T.B. UFFEN posted to Divison HQrs as 3rd Press Ambulance Lt #W ARMYTAGE appointed Acy: 4th (How) Bde RFA vice Capt A.S. ARCHDALE to Acy 15th & 73rd RFA	
"	27"		Orders received for 3 Bde RMA Q, Field Ambulances & Div. Field Coy A.s. to move from 14th Div. for fresh training from 26th. Casualties: 2nd Field Coy wnd OR 1, 6/S.Staff K OR 1, wnd OR 1, 5/N.Staff wnd OR 1, 6/N.Staff K OR 1, wnd OR 5, 5/Lincs K OR 1, wnd OR 8, 6/Sherwoods K OR 2, wnd OR 5, 8/Sherwoods wnd OR 1. Ammunition expended 13 pdr 23, 4.7" Lyd 19, 15 pdr 28, 5" How 14. Reinforcements: Capt W. MILNER 5/S.Staffs joined from BOULOGNE to rejoin. 2/Lt T. WEIR 109th Heavy Batty posted to 27th Bde Artillery.	
"	28		Carried out experiments with incendiary shells, but no useful results. Casualties: 6/N.Staffs K OR 1, wnd OR 3, 5/Lincs K OR 1, M OR 6 (Supposed lying out only) wnd OR 8, 6/Sherwoods K OR 1, wnd # OR 6, 7/Sherwoods K OR 1, 1st Field Ambulance wnd OR 1. Ammunition expended 13 pdr 17, 4.7" Lyd 3, Shrapnel 24, 15 pdr 44, 5" How 10. 3 Bdes 41st Bde (14th Divn) also 1 Field Amb. and 1 Coy of Train were attached to Div. for 14 days. 81st Bde marching through YPRES were billeted in LOCRE - DRANOUTRE Area. 1 R.C.D. 3 men (Chemical expert) attached to 2nd Field Coy, RE R.C. Chaplain MASON arrived and attached to 3rd Field Amb. Lt #W ARMYTAGE reported as Acy: 4/N.M. (How) Brigade. Brigade HQrs: NEUVE-EGLISE.	

WAR DIARY
or
INTELLIGENCE SUMMARY.
(Erase heading not required.)

Army Form C. 2118.

Place	Date	Hour	Summary of Events and Information	Remarks and references to Appendices
ST JANS CAPPEL	May 29		Major E.M. MORRIS B.M. Notts + Derby B.de appointed As command 2/R Inner Rifles. Capt W.G. NEILSON A v S Highlanders appointed B.de Major vice Major MORRIS Casualties 5/S Staff wnd OR 1, 6/S Staff wnd OR 2, 4/Lenics wnd OR 6, 5/Linc.K OR 1, wnd OR 3, 5/Lein wnd OR 1 (signally wd death). 6/Sherwoods wnd OR 1, 7/Sherwoods wnd Major B.E. BAILEY, OR 3 Ammunition expended 13 pdr 13, 4·7 Lyper 9, 15 pdr 39, 5" How 15 Vineyards reportedly reported on. Reinforcements 1 OR (AOC) left ROUEN at 22.45 on 28th Lieut H.W. ARMYTAGE named Rifleman Rulers of Regt. 4.2 (How) B.de R.F.A on 28th inst.	
"	May 30		Lieut BELLAIRS (tn spur) ordered to proceed home pesport dress of embarkation Casualties 5/S Staff wnd OR 1, 6/S Staff wnd OR 2, 5/N Staff wnd OR 6, 4/Lencs wnd OR 2, 5/Lincs.K OR 1 5/Sherwoods wnd OR 1, 6/Sherwoods K OR 1 wnd OR 3, 7/Sherwoods wnd OR 1 (slightly at duty) 8" K.R.R. wnd OR 3 Ammunition expended 13 pdr 20, 4·7 Lyger 37, 18 pdr 10, 15 pdr 35, 5" How 18 3 Howr Carts And 15 Cooker Carts - Complete Ammunition 29 limbers received as Ammunition 5 TR + 4 Turen Lords of 80" Inf B.de also 2 Turen Corp in LOCRE.DRANOUTRE Area Known wipr. Turday Thorpe (May 29) from 16803, Howns 4BSI.	Cash CRA 15 137 w/ 1 139 w/ 2 ———— 18
"	May 31		Casualties 5/S Staff wnd OR 1, 5/N Staff wnd OR 2, 8/Rifle Rg wnd OR 1, 5/Lancs wnd Lt C. O DIXON OR 2, 4/Lencs wnd Capt R.A FAIRE, 2 C J.G. ABELL, 5/Sherwoods wnd Lt H. CLAYE OR 1, 6/Sherwoods wnd 2/L G. GLOSSOP OR 5, 7/Sherwoods wnd OR 4, 8/K R R wnd 2/Lt A.G. WILLIAMS OR 2 Ammunition expended 13 pdr 17, 15 pdr 7 Capt F CAMPBELL-JOHNSON 2/Inn R.F.A posted As Sen. Information received from ROUEN that Major FULLER Missing - 2/Corps asked As cancel Capt Johnson's appointment 4·9 How. B.de. (No 1 B.4) Ordered As join Division - orders given As tak up positions on 2nd June. JMD	

46th Division

121/6073

Confidential

War Diary
of
46th (North Midland) Division (Administrative Branch)
from June 1st 1915 to June 30th 1915

(Volume IV)

WAR DIARY
or
INTELLIGENCE SUMMARY.

Army Form C. 2118.

Place	Date	Hour	Summary of Events and Information	Remarks and references to Appendices
ST JANS CAPPEL	June 1st		Capt BALL RE granted fortnight's leave. Casualties 5/N/Staffs wnded OR 1, 8/ Rifle Brigade wnded OR 1, 4/ Lincs wnded OR 1, 4/ Leics wnded OR 1, 5/Sherwoods wnded Major T.H.F MARSDEN OR 1, 6/Sherwoods wnded OR 1, 7/Sherwoods K OR 1 wnded OR 5, 8/KRR K OR 1. Lieut BELLAIRS Heavy Artillery embarked for ENGLAND. Ammunition expended 13 pdr 15, 4.7" Shrpnl 7, 15 pdr 6, 6" How 4. Orders called for Lt 4th Lt B Officers Selected for Assistance Aero be attached to Regular units. Capt W. G. NEILSON A.G.S Ardenman assuming duty of B.M. Major Notts & Derby Bde.	
	June 2nd		Reinforcements arrived 5/Lincs Officer 1, 1st Field Amb OR 2, 2nd Field Amb OR 7, 3rd Field Amb OR 6. Casualties 6/S. Staffs wnded OR 4, 5/N Staffs K OR 1 wnded OR 3, 6/N. Staffs wnded OR 1, 4/Leics K L.C.H. ELWOOD wnded OR 4, 4/Leics K OR 1, wnded OR 3, 7/Sherwoods wnded OR 1 (Slightly at duty) 8/KRR wnded OR 1, 2/Field Amb. wnded OR 1. 4th B. RHA returns to home early but any to join Cavalry tours – 49th B. RFA (How) leas 1 B. setting attached to Div from Army. Ammunition expended 13 pdr 11, 4.7" Lyddt 20, Shrpnl 7, 15 pdr 19, 5" How 16. Officers of 18th Division arrived for 3 days attachment.	
	June 3rd		Casualties C.S. Staffs wnded OR 1, 4/ Lincs wnded OR 1, 5/ Lincs K OR 1, 5/Sherwoods K OR 2, wnded L.M.S. FRYAR OR 4, 8/ Sherwoods wnded OR 3. Ammunition expended 4.7" Shrpnl 4, 15 pdr 17, 6" How 6, 15 pdr 40, 4.5" Lyddt 24 (Jun 12) (Jun 16) 4th B. RHA left having right of 2nd – 3rd. Names of Area Officers from each Brigade called for Machine Gun Course commencing on 7th inst.	

www.ingramcontent.com/pod-product-compliance
Lightning Source LLC
Chambersburg PA
CBHW081245170426
43191CB00034B/2043